**WEEK 1**

# LOOK AND SEE

# REFRAME YOUR VIEW

## WATCH

Watch Video Week 1, *Hidden in Plain Sight*, and record your personal thoughts as you listen.

## DISCUSS

In Luke 7, the overlooked woman behaved in a way that was culturally unacceptable for that time in history. She walked into a room of religious men and did the unthinkable. Not only did she let her hair down, which was so brazen it was considered grounds for divorce,[1] she also lavished expensive perfume on Jesus' feet, which was a bold act of love and humility.[2] As the religious men in the room judged her, Jesus turned toward the woman and asked His host, Simon, who was seated beside Him, "Do you see this woman?" (Luke 7:44).

Pause for a moment. Look over your notes. What stood out to you from the video teaching?

Have you ever felt invisible to someone? When has someone looked at you but not really seen you?

When that person looked at you but didn't see you, how did it make you feel? And how did you respond?

Why do you think Jesus asked Simon the question "Do you see this woman?" (Luke 7:44). What was He really asking Simon?

What do you think it means that "we often look but do not see"?

What may have blinded Simon from seeing the woman? What blinds us from really seeing people?

When Simon was face to face with Jesus—with God Himself—he didn't see Him! When he was beside Jesus looking at the woman, he didn't see her either. How is that even possible? There's something critical for us to learn about looking and seeing both people and God—and God in people.

**MOVE**

Consider the following action steps in response to what you've seen and heard today.

What did you learn through the experience of not being seen?

How has God used that experience to draw you to Himself and create in you a heart of compassion?

**PRAY**

Heavenly Father, open the eyes of my heart so that I'll see people and not overlook anyone. Help me to make those around me feel seen, known, heard, dignified, and valued. Use this study to show me how I can grow to see others more clearly. I want to see people the way You do. In Jesus' name. Amen.

# DAY 1

## *WHEN WE FEEL HIDDEN IN PLAIN SIGHT*

A number of years ago, when my daughters were young and we were traveling as a family, I decided to get a coffee right before we boarded. Checking the clock and the boarding time, I knew I had more than enough time for a coffee run. So off I went.

While I was gone, Nick decided to board with the girls and get them settled in with the games, toys, and books they had packed for the flight. Everything was running according to plan.

I made my way back to the gate with coffees in hand and time to spare. But when I started to pass from the terminal onto the jet bridge, the airline employee stationed at the doorway took one look at me and emphatically stated, "You're not getting on, ma'am."

Totally taken aback by her strong demeanor, I asked her what she meant. She said, "Well, if you have time to go and get coffee, then you don't have time to get on the plane."

I was shocked. It didn't make sense. I could see that the door to the plane was still open, and I knew it wasn't past the time to board, so I kindly said, "The door is open, ma'am. Please, take my boarding pass and let me board."

But she wouldn't budge.

"Ma'am, my husband and children are on board," I said. "I checked the time before I ran to get our coffee, and I knew I could make it back. Please let me on."

She was immovable.

She then began to review her day and all the challenging people she'd encountered. I politely agreed that she'd had a really tough day, but it still made no sense for me to be the object of her escalating frustration. I wasn't causing a problem. The door to the plane was still open. I had a reserved seat. Nick was waiting for me and was likely worried and wondering where I was.

As I started to tear up, I pleaded one more time, "Ma'am, my children are on the plane. Please, I can't let them leave without me. The door is still open. Please let me board."

I remember feeling so helpless, so surprised, so insignificant. I felt like she saw me as a problem, a nuisance, a bother ... not a human. Her actions made me feel like my request was invalid and my concerns for my family were unimportant. She was *looking* at me, but she wasn't *seeing* me. No matter how hard I tried, there was nothing I could say to make her see me.

I didn't want to make her bad day worse, but I had to get on that plane. As I wiped away a few tears with the back of my hand, my mother instincts kicked in to high gear. I found someone who had more authority than she did, and I got on that plane.

*How true that people may forget what we say or do, but they rarely forget how we make them feel.*

Even though that was years ago, I've never forgotten how that woman made me feel. Overlooked. Insignificant. Unseen. How true that people may forget what we say or do, but they rarely forget how we make them feel.

What about you? How many times has someone made you feel unseen or unheard? How many times have you felt categorized, marginalized, devalued, or dismissed because of your ethnicity or gender, because of your age or stage of life, because of your potential or education level? How many times have you felt overlooked for a job, an opportunity, or a promotion? How many times have you felt dismissed because of your role as a stay-at-home mom or a working mom, or because you never became a mom? What about when you wanted the attention of someone—a friend, a mentor, a spouse, or someone you were dating or hoped to date—and you felt invisible? What about the times you hoped to be picked first and were picked last, or not picked at all?

### un·seen

1.  not seen or noticed.
    synonyms: hidden, concealed, obscured, camouflaged, out of sight, invisible, imperceptible, undetectable, unnoticeable, unobserved, mysterious.[3]

Write about a time you felt overlooked or objectified in a situation.

What message did you hear about yourself when you were overlooked?

We've all known times when we've felt unseen. When someone else was chosen over us. When no one noticed our efforts or hard work. When no one noticed our passion or potential. When no one was empathetic to what we were going through. When someone looked right past us … or right through us. When it seemed they were looking our way but were incapable of seeing us—as though we were hidden in plain sight.

I'm so grateful God always looks right at us and sees us. None of us is ever unseen to God. He sees us no matter where we are or what we are doing. He sees our value and our worth. He sees our pain and our purpose. He sees our passion and potential. He sees our hearts and knows our deepest hopes, dreams, and desires. He never overlooks us or looks away from us. He looks right at us and sees us with 20/20 vision.

Look up the following verses and write how we know God sees us.

**Genesis 28:15**

**Psalm 32:8**

**Psalm 33:13-14**

**Proverbs 15:3**

When we are confident in knowing we are fully seen and fully known by God, we can see others and help them feel fully seen and fully known. When we aren't confident in knowing He sees us, we can be tempted to behave in a way that begs attention—whether negative or positive—hoping someone else will notice us. But if we spend most of our time doing things so we can be seen, we're apt to be tripping over the people we're meant to see. How crucial, then, to rest in knowing we are seen by God. To be seen and known by God fills our deepest longings. It is what we are looking for—whether we know it or not—and it is what helps us see others.

I'm well aware of the times I've acted more like the airline employee than like Jesus—when I've looked but not seen. How easy it is for us to absentmindedly look past our server in a restaurant, our manicurist at the salon, or the store clerk transacting our purchase. How common it is for us to stare at our phones and forget to look up and acknowledge the barista handing us our coffee.

> Make a list of people you typically interact with each week—in your neighborhood, at church, at the office, and so forth. If you don't know the person's name, just write a description of him or her.

*Looking* is not the same as *seeing*. To *look* is to "direct one's gaze in a specified direction."[4] To *see* is to "perceive with the eyes; discern visually."[5]

What a difference in meaning! The woman at the gate looked at me, but she didn't see me. She directed her gaze at me, but she didn't perceive or seem to fully understand my situation.

> Review the previous list. Ask God, "Who am I looking at regularly but not really seeing?" Circle anyone on the list He brings to mind.

> As you look at the names you circled, think about why you overlook them. Below, identify the reasons that apply to you or write others that come to mind.
> ☐ I'm too busy.
> ☐ I'm too tired.
> ☐ I'm focused on what I have to do.
> ☐ I'm in a rush.
> ☐ I have enough to think about with my own problems.
> ☐ I've been hurt and don't want to risk being hurt again.
> ☐ I don't want to intrude.

□ I think if they want my help, they'll ask for it

□ I feel awkward.

□ I don't feel comfortable with people who are different from me.

□ I don't believe it's my place to meddle.

□ Other:


Consider the reasons you just identified. Could you attribute any of those to a root issue listed below? To grow, we have to take an honest inventory of our hearts. Ask the Lord to show you if any of the following apply to you:

| | | |
|---|---|---|
| □ Selfishness | □ Fear | □ Pain |
| □ Greed | □ Indifference | □ Envy |
| □ Insecurity | □ Pride | □ Anger |
| □ Ignorance | □ Prejudice | □ Jealousy |
| □ Self-righteousness | | |

God wants us to look and see! And He wants us to take it a step further; He wants us to have 20/20 vision spiritually. He wants us to see and understand people with His perspective, especially those who cross our paths every day.

God has a lot to say in Scripture about spiritual sight. Look at the following verses and write what they say about how God sees.

1 Samuel 16:7

Isaiah 11:1-5

John 5:19

Look up the following verses and write down their implications for our spiritual sight.

2 Kings 6:15-17

Jeremiah 5:20-25

Ephesians 1:15-19a

1 Corinthians 2:6-16

Revelation 3:14-22

It's possible to look and not see. Read Proverbs 20:12 and fill in the blanks:

"The _____ and the _____, the LORD made them both."

This verse is true both physically and spiritually. Let's pray we are those who see the way He sees.

**ZOOM IN**
How many times have we missed important moments in our lives because we were too busy scrolling through someone else's?
It's time to look up and see who is right in front of us.

# DAY 2
## WHEN LENSES LIMIT

Jesus knows how we feel when people overlook us, look past us, or look right through us. He, too, was often overlooked by people who didn't see Him for who He really was. Many religious people—like the Pharisees and Sadducees—failed to see that He was the Son of God. They looked through lenses that limited their vision. In the video teaching, I mentioned that Simon sat and ate with Jesus and didn't even know who He was! He sat beside the Messiah, the Savior of the world, but Simon didn't see Him.

There was another time, after His resurrection, when Jesus wasn't recognized. This time, though, it wasn't His enemies or those who barely knew Him that didn't recognize Him; it was some who were closest to Him.

In Luke 24, two of Jesus' disciples were discouraged, because they didn't understand the redemptive mission of Jesus accomplished through His death, burial, and resurrection. They didn't realize He had to go to the Father in heaven so that the Holy Spirit could come and dwell in us on earth—that He had to fulfill all the prophecies we read today in the Old Testament. So, they left Jerusalem and headed out of town on the road to Emmaus.

Read Luke 24:13-35.

Did you notice all the times the words *eyes, look, seeing,* and *sight* were used? Did you notice how the two men were prevented from recognizing Jesus at first? Most scholars agree that they were divinely inhibited from recognizing Christ.[6] But their disappointment and disillusionment could have been a contributing factor to their spiritual blindness. They were so focused on their own pain. It was only after Jesus shared the scriptural narrative about Himself and broke bread with them that their fogged lenses cleared, and they recognized Him.

Although lenses are intended to correct our sight, they don't always work that way. Have you ever looked through a dirty windshield or a severely smudged pair of glasses? What happens? Everything you see becomes blurry at best and totally distorted at worst. Lenses can actually limit our sight, resulting in our failure to accurately see what's in front of us.

That's what happened with the two disciples and Simon the Pharisee. None of them were able to recognize Jesus.

What about you? Are your lenses blurred? What's preventing you from seeing Jesus? Disappointment or brokenheartedness? Self-righteousness?

Sadly, it wasn't uncommon in Jesus' day for people not to see Him for who He really was.

> Read the following Bible passages and answer these questions after each one: Who couldn't see Jesus? What clouded their spiritual lenses?
>
> Mark 6:1-6
>
> Mark 8:27-30
>
> John 18:28-40
>
> John 21:1-14

I have often wondered what Jesus was like in His growing-up years. Was He playful, funny? When He was a toddler, did He spit out His lentils and make His mother laugh? As He grew older, was He responsible and helpful with His younger siblings? Firstborns often are. If Mary and Joseph were keenly aware of who He really was, how did they juggle knowing He was so incredibly special with letting Him just be a boy who caught bugs and played with His brothers and sisters?

I don't know all the answers to my musings, but I find one story in the Bible very insightful. It's a story that unfolds around the time Jesus was entering young adulthood and His identity wasn't recognized.

> Read Luke 2:41-52.

Can you believe it? Mary is recorded forever in the Holy Bible as having left a kid behind while returning home from a family vacation! Mary lost Jesus—not for one hour, or two hours, or even a full day, but for three full days! This passage should free of guilt every mother who has ever been late for pick-up, left a kid

at school, or lost a kid at a grocery store. And, it should make this the best Bible study you've ever walked through!

OK, back to the main point. Mary and Joseph assumed Jesus was somewhere in the large traveling party. That's why they didn't start looking for Him until after a full day had passed. But when they realized He was missing, they immediately launched a full-scale search. They finally found Him in Jerusalem, teaching adults in the temple.

How did the people who were listening to Jesus in the temple react to His teachings?

Do you think they were able to see who He really was? Explain.

When Mary and Joseph approached Jesus, Mary wanted to know why He had been so insensitive to them, why He didn't think about how His disappearing act would affect them. She acted just like any parent would, and though He gave a sincere answer, they didn't understand His reasoning.

What does this story reveal about how Joseph and Mary saw Jesus? What may have been limiting the lens through which they saw Him?

How often do we—like Simon, Mary Magdalene, the people in the temple, the people in the synagogue, and Mary and Joseph—miss seeing Jesus for who He really is because our lenses are unclear? We often allow them to become smudged and clouded by our feelings, circumstances, or other distractions.

Take some time to reflect on the reasons that contributed to unclear lenses for everyone we've mentioned. Which of those reasons—or other feelings, circumstances, and distractions—may be distorting your vision of Jesus or causing you to overlook Him for who He really is?

When our lenses are clear—when our hearts and minds are open—we see the presence of Jesus everywhere.

Let's make one more application point today. When I think about how Joseph and Mary thought Jesus was being looked after by someone else in the large traveling party, I can't help but consider that perhaps we don't look and see others because we think someone else is.

In the context of our study, can you think of anyone you've looked past because you thought someone else was seeing them?

Today, make it a point to have clean and clear lenses so your vision isn't limited, so you can see Jesus and everyone around you, especially those you might normally overlook.

# DAY 3

## *WHEN BEAMS BLIND*

Can you imagine being in the presence of God and being oblivious to Him? Isn't that what Simon did? And the people in the temple and synagogue? I think it's fascinating that Jesus was often unseen by people. And yet, He always saw the one—the person He was meant to acknowledge, notice, speak to, or heal. He saw the grieving widow from Nain who lost her only son (Luke 7:11-15), Zacchaeus up in the tree (Luke 19:1-10), and the disabled man at the pool of Bethesda (John 5:1-9).

> Read John 5:19-23. According to this passage, how did Jesus know the one who needed to be seen in each situation? How does this apply to us?

In the Gospel of Mark, there is a story of a blind man who was brought to Jesus. On the day Jesus entered his life, this blind man was the one. Before we walk through this story, I want to point out the significance of its placement in Mark's Gospel and in the lives of Jesus' disciples.

My friend and fellow LifeWay author, Lisa Harper, noted in her Bible study, *The Gospel of Mark,* that the first half of Mark's Gospel (Mark 1:1–8:30) is all about the compassion of Jesus Christ, while the second half (Mark 8:31–16:8) is all about the passion of Jesus Christ—His unwavering commitment to fulfill His sacrificial calling to the cross.[7]

The story I want us to look at is placed right in the middle of Mark's Gospel—in the center of this transition of focus. It's preceded by Jesus feeding four thousand people because He was moved with compassion (Mark 8:2), after which  He got into a boat and headed to the district of Dalmanutha (Mark 8:10). There, the Pharisees showed up and began to argue with Him.

> Read Mark 8:11-21 and note what Jesus asked His disciples in verse 18. What did He mean?

Immediately following Jesus' conversation with His disciples is the story of the blind man who was brought to Jesus. This can't be a coincidence! Is Jesus teaching us just like He taught His disciples?

Read Mark 8:22-25.

Let's look at what stands out as unusual about this story, apart from Jesus spitting on a man's eyes. And let me just say, that's always the part of the story that stops me in my tracks. I'm such a germaphobe I can barely read this story without cringing. I guess sometimes you have to receive God's healing however it comes, but it would take some work for me to get past the spit!

Here's my question: Why did Jesus lay hands on him not once, but twice? Surely, His healing power wasn't wearing off! What was really going on?

After Jesus touched him the first time, what did the blind man see? What about after the second time?

In the story of Jesus healing the blind man, the man doesn't receive his sight immediately. Instead, it seems to be a two-step process.

To dig into why that might be, let's review the following verses and note whether they are talking about spiritual or physical blindness.

Jeremiah 5:21

Ezekiel 12:2

Matthew 13:10-16

Which kind of blindness was the man healed from? Spiritual, physical, or both?

Read Mark 8:27-29. How does the man's experience compare to how the disciples saw Jesus—both before this story and after?

Jesus' gift of spiritual and physical sight to the blind man was symbolic of the disciples' spiritual progression. Before this healing story, the disciples were confused about who Jesus was and what His purpose was, and Jesus challenged them on it in Mark 8:14-21. But following the miracle, their vision began to clear. Like the blind man, they needed a second touch. They had experienced some spiritual insight in their time with Jesus but it wasn't yet complete.[8]

Are there areas in your life where you've gone from spiritual blindness to spiritual sight? Did it happen immediately? Or in stages? Describe the process.

Learning to look and really see is a process, a journey that God will take us on through this study. And I believe as we earnestly seek Him, He will do a work in us internally to prepare us to do a work for Him externally. Isn't that the kind of transformation He was working in His disciples' hearts and minds? He was maturing them so they wouldn't just look, but see clearly. Focused. With understanding as they went through life.

*He will do a work in us internally to prepare us to do a work for Him externally.*

In John 9, Jesus healed another blind man who was born without his sight, and He did so on the Sabbath. The Pharisees investigated the miracle, because they believed it was unlawful for Jesus to heal on their holy day.

You can read the entire account in John 9, but I want you to write below the question the Pharisees asked Jesus (v. 40), and how Jesus answered them (v. 41).

From Jesus' response, it seems the Pharisees thought they knew and saw everything, but they were more blind than the man who was healed. They couldn't see the one Man or the miracle. Like Simon the Pharisee, who couldn't see Jesus for who He really was or the woman sitting at Jesus' feet, they were blinded by their self-righteousness.

## blind

1. unable to see.
   synonyms: sightless, unsighted, visually impaired, visionless, unseeing

2. lacking perception, awareness, or discernment.

3. cause (someone) to be unable to see, permanently or temporarily.

4. deprive (someone) of understanding, judgment, or perception.[9]

Jesus addressed the condition of being spiritually blind more than once.

Read Matthew 7:1-5.

Oftentimes, we don't see people because we're blinded by the beam of wood in our own eyes, which makes it easy to become judgmental. That's what the Pharisees' self-righteousness was—a beam. I contend that we grow so accustomed to having beams in our eyes that we are often unaware of them. We need to regularly ask the Holy Spirit to reveal the beams to us.

I love praying Psalm 139:23-24:

Search my heart, God, and know my heart;
test me and know my concerns.
See if there is any offensive way in me;
lead me in the everlasting way.

When I pray these verses, God is faithful to show me when I've been frustrated with someone because of a beam in my own eye—sometimes one of judgment or unforgiveness. God wants us to keep our hearts open to hearing what He has to say so our hearts can stay free and our sight can stay clear.

When have you focused on others' splinters and judged them, even though you had to look around a beam in your own eye to see them?

What motivated you to be judgmental? What was the beam in your eye? Label it. Anger? Jealousy? Prejudice? Selfish ambition? Competition? Insecurity? Pride? Self-righteousness?

In Luke 18, Jesus told a parable to make a point about those who looked down on others because they trusted in their own righteousness.

Read Luke 18:9-14. How can you begin the process of going from looking to seeing without a beam in your eye?

Write a prayer asking God to remove the beam you identified earlier.

God wants us to see, but He also wants us to understand that sight is more than what the eye sees; it's what the heart sees and perceives, free of judgment. Think about those you have judged wrongly, and make it a point to see them and love them with a new perspective. See them as the one.

# DAY 4

## *JESUS SAW THROUGH THE LENS OF COMPASSION*

When my mum was in the later years of her life, her health began to decline and her memory started to fail. It was sad for my brothers and me to see our roles reverse from being cared for to being caregivers. In the last two years of her life, her need for assistance intensified.

Though my brothers and I offered to get her an in-home full-time caregiver, she didn't want one. She was also unwilling to move to a safer place that offered around-the-clock care. She wanted to maintain her independence at all costs, even though it was becoming increasingly unsafe and unwise. For my brothers and me, it was agonizing—and at times beyond frustrating—because no matter what we said, Mum couldn't see our point of view. She refused to acknowledge what we all saw.

So many times I wanted to throw my hands up in the air in frustration and get back on a plane to America where I could be far away from my mum's suffering—because, let's be honest, sometimes it's easier to be compassionate with people who are far away from us than with the ones who are up close.

*If we focus on protecting ourselves, we will miss others.*

How essential it is, then, that we come before Jesus daily and ask Him to keep the eyes of our hearts open so we can see those closest to us in the same way He does. When we feel rejected or taken for granted by our husbands, children, friends, or colleagues, we can easily default to a defensive posture and harden our hearts to shield us from being hurt. But if we allow our hearts to harden, then we will lose compassion and, there-fore, lack what is required to see others as Jesus does. If we focus on protecting ourselves, we will miss others.

When my conversations with Mum grew difficult and she became upset, she wasn't trying to hurt me. She was simply frightened. She didn't want to leave the home where she'd lived for more than forty years. The home where she raised us kids and spoiled her grandkids. The home where decades of memories resided. She didn't want to move and be dependent upon someone else. She had always been such a strong person. Even as a teen, she boarded a ship in Egypt with her sister and set sail for Australia. They were escaping political upheaval in Egypt, and her parents had only enough money to buy passage for the two of them. In Australia, she managed to secure a job, save money, and send for her parents and younger brother so they could be together again. I always found that extraordinary. She had spent her entire life in Australia as an immigrant working to build a life and look after her family.

When I considered her life—the obstacles she overcame, the tragedies she endured, and the sacrifices she made for all of us—I understood her reluctance to leave her home. When I saw her perspective, my frustration melted into love.

When I just loved her and stopped feeling discouraged or frustrated with her, our time was filled with laughing and sharing good memories. I definitely had to rely on the wisdom and strength of the Holy Spirit to navigate through that difficult season, but I am so grateful my brothers and I persevered. My final year with her had so many happy moments—all because I chose to love her and see her through the lens of compassion.

We view people through the lens of compassion when we see them for who they really are and are deeply moved to respond.

Jesus always saw the one, and when He did, the Gospels often say He was moved with compassion. Jesus saw people and felt their pain, loneliness, misery, hopelessness, and desperation—even when it was hidden in plain sight from everyone else.

The Greek verb translated "had compassion" or "moved with compassion" in the Gospels is the word *splagchnizomai*. It means to be deeply moved in the inward parts, in one's bowels. Today, we might say it means to be so moved we feel it in our core, deep within ourselves—in our gut. But to feel compassion is not only to encounter an emotion, it's to be moved to action.[10]

Read the following verses and list who Jesus saw through the lens of compassion and how He expressed that compassion.

Matthew 14:14

Matthew 15:32-39

Matthew 20:29-34

Mark 6:34

Seeing through the lens of compassion changes our view of people. It enables us to see who they really are and respond.

I'll never forget the time when Sophia was little and she got away from me on a busy street. I was holding her hand as we raced from place to place getting errands accomplished. But all of a sudden, I realized her hand was no longer in mine. When I looked down and back through the crowd, desperate for a glimpse of her sweet face, she was crouched down in front of a homeless man handing him the dollar bill I had given her that morning. She had been so indecisive at every stop we'd made, debating on how to spend it. On a trinket? A piece of candy? A toy? And there she was just handing it over to this man. She said, "Jesus gave me this dollar to give to you."

Then I watched as the man gave it back, and with tears streaming down his face, he said, "Honey, you spend it on some candy for yourself."

Sophia gave him something far more valuable than a dollar. She extended to him a heart full of compassion.

I was beyond relieved to find her and overwhelmed at the goodness of God in her. I was grateful she wasn't numb to someone who was asking for help. I have always wanted my girls' eyes to be open to really see people and to be moved to act with compassion. Sophia was moved that day, and I was so grateful.

Look up the following verses and notice where compassion comes from and what we're to do with it.

Colossians 3:12

2 Corinthians 1:3-4

When did you last feel compassion? What did it move you to do?

How did compassion affect your sight and change your perception of someone else?

When our compassion wears thin, we can develop "compassion fatigue." This term isn't in the Bible, and I doubt they had such a term in Jesus' day, but it's a very real condition. It happens when we give out of our hearts so long that we are no longer moved with tenderness and empathy, and we no longer feel or see like Jesus does.

## com·pas·sion fa·tigue

1. indifference to charitable appeals on behalf of those who are suffering, experienced as a result of the frequency or number of such appeals.[11]

When Jesus felt depleted—because even though He was God, He was also fully man (Phil. 2:5-8; Col. 2:9; 1 John 4:2-3) and felt all the same things we do (Heb. 4:15)—He took steps to maintain the ability to see the one through the lens of compassion.

Read the following verses and write what Jesus did to avoid compassion fatigue. Note how He found rest and solitude to replenish His soul.

Mark 1:35; 6:30-32

Luke 5:15-16; 6:12-13

In the work of A21, the anti-trafficking organization Nick and I founded, our team sees the pain and suffering of victims up close.[12] To ensure everyone stays mentally and emotionally healthy, we watch team members closely so we can respond when signs of compassion fatigue surface. Notice I said "when," not "if."

Compassion fatigue is inevitable in so many seasons of our lives:

- When our children are small and we feel overwhelmed trying to juggle the roles of wife, mother, friend, colleague, and employee.
- When our kids are older and we're out every night of the week attending games or parent meetings and grabbing dinner on the go.

- When we're building our careers, putting in long hours, developing teams, and leading new growth.

- When we decide to go back to school while working and raising a family.

- When we're a long-term caregiver for a child or aging parent.

Signs of compassion fatigue can include physical, mental, and spiritual exhaustion; acute emotional pain; growing less empathetic; withdrawing from others.

It's surprising how what comes into our lives as a gift—raising a family, an outreach opportunity, caregiving, a new friend, starting a business, and even our phones—can evolve into a source of exhaustion, draining away all of the tenderness, sensitivity, and enthusiasm we once had. And because of that, we can go from truly seeing people to overlooking them everywhere we go—all because we're bone tired.

> Consider the last few months of your life. Have you experienced any signs of compassion fatigue? Circle any of the following behaviors, thoughts, or habits that have crept into your life.
>
> ☐ Feeling hopeless
> ☐ Growing fearful
> ☐ Wrestling through sleepless nights
> ☐ Being attacked with anxiety
> ☐ Experiencing headaches
> ☐ Feeling depressed
> ☐ Feeling angry
> ☐ Growing pessimistic or cynical
> ☐ Becoming overly vigilant about safety
> ☐ Feeling people have become an inconvenience

If you are suffering from compassion fatigue, please don't withdraw or feel like you can't tell anyone. Reach out to a Christian friend or mentor and share what you are feeling. Ask them to pray with you and walk with you through the process of healing. Take time to reflect, rest, and replenish. Seek professional help if you need it—I firmly believe in the benefits of sound Christian counseling. I strongly encourage you to ask for help.

# DAY 5
## *EYES WIDE OPEN!*

My girls are both in their teens now, and that means they sleep. A lot. By the time they get up on a Saturday, I've had coffee, gone for a run, eaten lunch, and run errands! Yes, it's afternoon by the time they begin to stir.

They not only sleep a lot, they sleep like rocks. Even when our dog, Ezra Blake, who sleeps on Sophia's bed, snores so loudly that it sounds like a freight train, both girls sleep right through it. I guess to them it must sound like a lullaby!

But when it's a school day, well, that's a different story. Both girls have to set their alarms and get up on time. Of course, Nick and I serve as the backup system. We stop by their doors, listen for sounds of life, and take the necessary steps to ensure they are getting ready.

Sometimes when we listen at their bedroom doors we don't hear anything. Not a peep. That's when we enter their rooms and shake them awake!

Perhaps that's what God has been doing in us all week. Shaking us awake. Moving us from a place of blurry-eyed sleepiness to fully opening our eyes so we can see the people around us the way He does—without prejudice, without objectifying them, without dismissing them.

Even the Christians in the Ephesian church fell asleep, and the apostle Paul had to shake them awake!

Read Ephesians 5:1 and write the first instruction.

What a powerful command! Paul told the Ephesians that God wanted them to imitate Him—and then he listed multiple ways they were to do so. But near the end of that list, in verse 14, he told them that part of imitating God is being awake, eyes wide open.

Read Ephesians 5:8-15, paying special attention to verse 14. Why is it so important to stay spiritually awake?

When I read Ephesians 5:14, it occurs to me that it's possible to go through life asleep—fully functioning but not fully awake. I'd call that sleepwalking! God doesn't want us sleepwalking through life. If we do, we will miss everyone He wants us to see. Besides, sleepwalking is dangerous.

*God doesn't want us sleepwalking through life.*

Our eldest, Catherine, has had episodes of sleepwalking, so much so that we had to put a special door upstairs so she wouldn't sleepwalk downstairs, open the front door, and walk out. In the course of researching her experiences, I've learned a lot about sleepwalking. Did you know that sleepwalkers remain in a deep sleep throughout their episodes, making them unlikely to remember anything? And oftentimes sleepwalking involves more than just walking. People who sleepwalk have been known to try to drive a car or perform other activities that can be dangerous to themselves or others. Also, it's a common belief that sleepwalkers should not be awakened; however, research says it can be more dangerous to allow a sleepwalker to stay asleep than to wake them—especially if they are attempting to drive a car![13]

All of this tells me that sleepwalking, physically or spiritually, is not a good idea!

Describe what sleepwalking spiritually might look like in your life.

In Mark 13:32-37, Jesus taught His disciples about His second coming. He warned them three times to "stay awake" or "be alert." Could it be He didn't want them spiritually sleepwalking?

Read Mark 13:32-37 and note the three times Jesus instructed His disciples to remain awake.

If Jesus told the disciples—and us—something three times in the same breath, then could it be that He wants us to understand more than the obvious? If we keep reading in Mark we learn that a couple days after Jesus told them to stay awake, He ate with His disciples at the last supper, and then, together, they went to the garden of Gethsemane for Jesus to pray.

Matthew, Mark, and Luke all record aspects of this night. Read the account in Matthew 26:36-46, and note the disciples' actions and Jesus' words to them.

The disciples couldn't stay awake for one hour, even after Jesus asked them a second time. He didn't bother to wake them again, and they slept through His greatest agony. Can you imagine sleeping through a moment God invited you into? And then that moment becoming one of the most pivotal in history?

That's the danger God wants us all to avoid. We don't want to sleep through the moments He invites us into, the ones He's orchestrated into every one of our days. How important it is for us to look and see, to be alert and awake, to see the one God wants us to see.

When has God invited you to look and see someone as He does? Describe that moment and how you responded.

Based on what we've studied this week about looking and seeing, about feeling seen and then helping others feel seen, do you think it's possible for us to be so drained from our own disappointments and circumstances that we "fall asleep" spiritually while still going through the motions of our everyday lives? Explain.

How can falling asleep spiritually affect our vision?

Could it be that we're spiritually sleepwalking? We're functioning, yet we're going through life with our eyes closed, blind to everyone around us. We may even be blind to Jesus.

God's words to the disciples and to the Ephesians to "Wake up!" and "Be alert!" roughly two thousand years ago are still true for us today.

Here are some verses that reiterate this very message. Look them up and write what stands out to you.

Deuteronomy 4:9

Luke 12:35-38

Romans 13:11-12

Ephesians 6:18

1 Thessalonians 5:1-8

1 Peter 5:8

Revelation 3:1-3

Revelation 3:14-22

God is calling us to wake up and to open our eyes wide—our physical eyes so we can see people, and our spiritual eyes so we can *really see* people.

Choose a Scripture passage from the list above and write it as a prayer, asking God to help you be alert, stay awake, and have 20/20 vision.

WEEK 2

# GO AND TELL

# REFRAME YOUR VIEW

## WATCH

Watch Video Week 2, *Be a God Carrier*, and record your personal thoughts as you listen.

_____

_____

_____

_____

_____

_____

_____

_____

_____

_____

_____

_____

_____

_____

_____

_____

_____

## DISCUSS

Mary was an ordinary teenage girl—wholesome, Jewish, and betrothed to a young man named Joseph. She was a virgin. She was going about her normal, everyday life when God interrupted with startling news—she was to carry the Son of God and bring Him into the world. Just like God chose Mary to carry Jesus to her world, He's chosen us to carry Jesus to our world. He interrupts our lives—and everything that we have planned—to invite us to fulfill His purpose.

Pause for a moment. Look over your notes. What stood out to you from the video teaching?

What do you think it means to be a God-carrier to your generation?

How have you seen God use ordinary people to do extraordinary things? Has God used you in that way? Explain.

What does it mean to have God's favor for purpose, not for status?

When has God's purpose interrupted your plans?

How have you allowed fear to keep you from moving forward with God?

"If we are going to step out in faith and carry God to our world, then we must learn to replace what we do not know about the future with what we do know about God." What does this statement mean, and how do we daily live it out?

What God-sized challenges are you facing right now? Are you facing them in fear or faith?

Matthew 28:18-20 records the last words Jesus spoke before He ascended to heaven: "Jesus came near and said to them, 'All authority has been given to me in heaven and on earth. Go, therefore, and make disciples of all nations, baptizing them in the name of the Father and of the Son and of the Holy Spirit, teaching them to observe everything I have commanded you. And remember, I am with you always, to the end of the age.'"

Last words are some of the most important words someone can speak to us. I'll always treasure my own mother's last words to me. My brother helped her FaceTime with me, and I remember looking at her sweet smile and hearing her say, "I love you."

Jesus had been away from heaven for thirty-three years, and on His way home, He paused to give us His last words: "Go and make disciples ..." I believe it's time we make Jesus' last command our greatest priority. I believe it's time we fully understand that He has seen us, chosen us, and sent us.

## MOVE

How is God calling you to carry Him to your generation? What does that look like for you?

What specific action steps do you need to take to fulfill this calling?

## PRAY

God, thank You for choosing me to carry Your Son, Jesus, to my world. Although I don't always feel adequate or fully understand how to do this, I pray You will give me the strength and courage to not only see others as You see them, but to actually step out in faith and reach them with Your love. I want to carry You into my sphere of influence in a manner worthy of the gospel. I choose to say yes.

# DAY 1

## *WE ARE CHOSEN*

"Christine?" Mum asked. "Since we're telling the truth, would you like to know the whole truth?"

I was thirty-three years old at the time. I had raced over to her house to intervene in what I just knew couldn't be true. My brother, George, had received a letter from Social Services saying he was adopted and that his birth mother wanted to contact him. I walked in Mum's front door just as George was handing her that letter.

I'll never forget the way her hands started to shake. The fear that filled her eyes. The loss of words. The tears that began to flow endlessly, from us all—George and his wife, Kathy, Mum, and me. She really didn't need to read the letter. She already knew what was in it.

When she finally found her voice, I could hear her heart breaking. "I'm so sorry you found out like this, George. We never meant to hurt you. Your dad loved you. I love you. I couldn't love you more if I'd given birth to you myself."

As her words kept tumbling out, we could only listen. Dad made her promise never to tell. They agreed it was best. They wanted George to have a wonderful life, knowing he was fully loved, fully wanted—without an inkling of rejection. Her words were so beautiful, loving, and sincere. So full of devotion.

I remember heading into the kitchen and spreading the table with food, because there's one way Greek families solve every kind of problem—we eat. As we all moved toward the table—the same table where George and I and our younger brother, Andrew, did our homework, played board games, and laughed and joked for decades—Mum shared more of the story. The more she talked, the more she seemed relieved of this terrible, weighty burden, and it helped us to begin wrapping our minds around what seemed so inconceivable.

It was when I reached for the baklava that Mum asked that all-telling question, and somehow, I knew. Searching her eyes for the answer, wanting it to be anything other than what I was thinking, I found myself saying it for her: "I was adopted too."

I was a grown, married woman, thirty-three years old, and I was learning for the first time that I wasn't who I thought I was. I wondered what else wasn't real. How many more secrets were there?

The funny thing is, of all the things that could have popped into my head and out my mouth, I asked, "Am I still Greek?"

It was the comic relief we all needed on one of the toughest days of our lives together. And what I said next astounded me even more, but it reflected the previous decade of my life—years in which I'd spent time learning the Word, renewing my mind, and giving all my heart to Jesus.

"Before I was formed in my mother's womb"—and I paused to add, "whosever womb that was—God knew me. He knit together my innermost parts and fashioned all of my days before there was even one of them. I am fearfully and wonderfully made. Even though I've only just found out I was adopted, God has always known, and He has always loved me. And since that hasn't changed, nothing has changed. I may not be who I thought I was, but I still am who He says I am. And I am more. I am loved. I am His."

My mum, brother, and sister-in-law were as shocked as I was by what I said, but it was *the truth*. And it would serve to be the foundation of how I would move through the months ahead—sorting out my heart, helping George sort out his heart, and comprehending all that our parents had kept from both of us.

That day, somewhere in the middle of all Mum told us, somewhere in the middle of sharing the memories of trying to conceive for years and then being given the opportunity to adopt, she said the most beautiful words to us. Words that brought such healing. She even repeated them to me in the weeks following:

"I loved you before I knew you."

To this day, I cherish those words. They were the heart of a mother letting me know that she longed for me, wanted me, and chose me even before she ever laid eyes on me.

When I think of those words, I can't help but hear the heart of my heavenly Father, the One who has always wanted me too. The One who chose me long before my mother did.[14]

> When was the last time you were chosen for something? Were you invited to join a committee? Invited by a new friend to dinner? Picked for a city sports team? Asked to give a talk? How did it make you feel to be chosen?

That positive feeling is only a fraction of the joy and peace God wants us to experience in knowing that we are chosen. This truth is so important God had it explicitly written on the pages of Scripture so we could never forget.

> Read Ephesians 1:3-6 and personalize what God did for you that He never wants you to forget.

## cho·sen

1. having been selected as the best or most appropriate.
synonyms: selected, picked, appointed, elected, favored, hand-picked[15]

Did you notice in the definition of *chosen* that one of the synonyms is "favored"? That's what the angel said to Mary: "Greetings, favored woman! The Lord is with you" (Luke 1:28). Mary was chosen.

Being chosen by God isn't something we have to compete for or strive for. Unlike the performance-driven world in which we live, God doesn't choose us based on who's the most popular, gifted, talented, wealthy, educated, connected, or perfect. He chooses each of us just the way He created us.

*Being chosen by God isn't something we have to compete for or strive for.*

> Look up John 15:16a and write what it says in the space provided below.

Read the following verses and record how God describes our relationship to Him once He has chosen us.

John 1:12

Romans 8:16-17

1 John 3:1

God has chosen us to be His daughters, and being His daughters comes with so many privileges: We are forgiven, healed, transformed, redeemed, and restored. We are put on the path to fulfilling our purpose and potential.

And all for a very important reason.

If we were chosen simply so we could go to heaven and be with Jesus for all eternity, then we would be there already. But God has chosen to leave us in the here and now, for now. Why doesn't He take us home the minute we say yes to Jesus? Because there is something He wants done in the here and now, right now.

Read Colossians 1:27-29. What was Paul's charge and how was he fulfilling it? How does that apply to us?

God entrusted Jesus to Mary, and He has entrusted Jesus to us. What a gift! We are flawed people who carry an indwelling Lord. God the Son lives in us through the Holy Spirit. We are a habitat of all the fullness of the living God (Eph. 3:19). That is the glory of the gospel, one of its mysteries.

My daughter, Catherine, loves playing volleyball. She practices year-round, all in the hope of being chosen for the school's team each fall. Like most high school sports, it's highly competitive, and as the girls go through tryouts they all wonder if they'll make the team and which team they'll make: varsity or junior varsity.

We've been through this season enough times now that I don't need a calendar to tell you what time of year it is—I can sense the tension in our home. Catherine feels the most pressure, but sometimes it feels like we're all trying out for the team! I often remind her (and myself) of the peace we have in Christ.

Thankfully, when it comes to God's team, we don't have to go through tryouts, and we don't have to live fearful that we won't make the cut.

Because of Christ we have a place on God's team. And it's not to warm the bench; it's to be in the starting lineup. Not convinced? We are saved to do good works (Eph. 2:8-10). We are supernaturally gifted to carry out the work of ministry (1 Cor. 12; Rom. 12:5-8). We are called to run the race with endurance that Christ has given us (Heb. 12:1-2).

Being on a team comes with expectations. Once Catherine is on a team, she's expected to be an active, engaged member. She's expected to be at every practice and game, to listen to her coach, to study the playbook, to encourage her teammates, and to celebrate every individual achievement and team win. In short, she's expected to be a volleyball player in every way—mentally, emotionally, and physically.

God has expectations of us as members of His team.

Read John 15:16. What does God expect of us?

In light of our discussion, what do you think it means to bear fruit?

When Catherine makes the team each year, they give her a new uniform. It has her name and number on it, and it signifies which team she's a part of.

As chosen members of God's team, we have been given a new uniform. God wants us to take off our old "clothes" and put on the new ones He's given us.

Read Colossians 3:5-10 and write what God wants us to "put off."

Now read Colossians 3:12-17 and record what He wants us to "put on."

Who needs you to show them more compassion, kindness, humility, gentleness, and patience?

How can you begin to cultivate a greater depth of these qualities in your life and express them to those around you?

The Greek word for "chosen" used in Colossians 3:12 is *eklektos*. It signifies being picked out, selected.[16] It's an intentional choice. What other words does God call us in Colossians 3:12?

**ZOOM IN**

Some translations say "holy and dearly loved;" others say "holy and beloved." Both are beautiful. The word "beloved" comes from the Greek word *agapao*, which comes from *agape*, meaning "love." The tense used in Colossians 3:12 is significant, because it means "God has loved us in the past; He still loves us in the present; and He will continue to love us in the future."[17]

God has loved us and will love us for all eternity. His love for us is unending, never failing, and all-encompassing. He is faithful, loyal, and steadfast.

Look up Hebrews 13:8 and write it in the space provided below. Let it become life to your heart.

God has chosen us for His plan. Read 1 Peter 2:9. Fill in the names that God calls us.

1. A chosen _____

2. A royal _____

3. A holy _____

4. A _____ for His _____

What does verse 9 say we are called out to do?

God sees you. He has chosen you. You are His loved daughter and a starter on His team. You are to bear fruit and proclaim His praises—the One who has called you out of the darkness and into His marvelous light. Believing these truths is the first step to seeing and serving others, to carrying God to your world.

# DAY 2

## *WE ARE SENT*

When I first moved to the United States, I would call my mum frequently to stay in touch. But because of the time difference and our busy schedules, it was sometimes challenging to connect. When it was my daytime, it was her nighttime. When I was sitting in an airport with free time, she was at bingo night—something no one could interrupt!

When I suggested emailing or FaceTiming or texting to keep up with each other, she acted like I was from Mars. She wasn't part of the iPhone generation and was terrified of our modern communication methods.

So, I resorted to one of the oldest methods of communication possible—letters. Yes, I stepped back in time and wrote letters to my mum.

In case you're too young to know what letters are, they are hand-written notes comprised of much longer sentences than found in a text. They are written with a pen filled with ink, often on a type of paper referred to as "stationary," although you can hand-write a note on any piece of paper. In a traditional letter, you express your personal thoughts and feelings, often telling the recipient of the latest happenings, describing them in great detail. Without emojis. Once you write a letter on stationary or in a greeting card, you place it in an envelope. Then you seal it, address it, put a stamp on it, and mail it.

I should probably sit down with my daughters for a tutorial on this because now that I'm explaining it all to you, I'm not sure they would know what I'm talking about. And this might be a good time, if you're in a group Bible study, to invoke the instructions of Titus 2:3-5, where the older women are to teach the younger. I'm sure Paul just accidently left out letter-writing mentoring in his instructions.

Because of the distance between my mum and me, by the time she got my letters, at least a week had passed. Can you imagine how old all of my news was? By the time Mum found out Catherine had a recital and Sophia had learned to ride a bike, our family had lived at least seven more days of adventure.

But sometimes, the letters were lost and she never received them at all.

Can you remember a time you sent a letter and it didn't arrive when it should have? Or worse, it got lost forever? How long did it take for the letter to arrive, if it arrived at all? How did you feel?

Read 2 Corinthians 3:1-3. How does Paul describe the Corinthian believers in verses 2-3?

How were the letters written? Who read them?

To understand the context, Paul was defending himself and his apostleship against opponents who were accusing him of duplicity and insincerity. In trying to defend himself, he anticipated they would also accuse him of arrogance. But Paul countered in verse 1 that he didn't need to commend himself with "letters of recommendation." He was referring to a practice whereby traveling Christians would carry with them a letter of recommendation that spoke of their good standing in their church. They would use this letter to introduce themselves to congregations that didn't know them.[18] Paul said he didn't need that kind of commendation because the transformed hearts and lives of the Corinthian believers proved the authenticity of his ministry. They were "Christ's letter ... not written with ink but with the Spirit of the living God" (v. 3). And their changed lives were on display for all to see.

Just as the Corinthians were Christ's letters, so are we. I find this analogy very telling because letters carry messages. Isn't that what my letters to Mum carried? Think about the last time you wrote a "Dear John" letter. (You have written at least one of those, right? No? Please don't tell me you dumped him with a text.)

Letters are often filled with heart-felt words of condolences, congratulations, or enduring commitment.

As letters of Christ, what is the message we are to carry? Read
1 Corinthians 15:1-4 and summarize your answer.

To whom are we to carry this message? Read Mark 16:15 and
John 17:15-19 and write your findings below.

*God didn't send
a text message or
social media post
to the world. He
sent us.*

Those last two verses speak deeply to me. I believe the most
important word in Mark 16:15 is *go*. It's two-thirds of how we
spell God's name! He wants us to go … into the world, to
love and understand the lost, to have compassion on them.
He wants us to go and tell. Then, John 17:15-19 makes it
even more clear: "As you sent me, I send them …" Jesus has
sent us to a lost and broken world in desperate need of the
gospel message God has chosen to deliver through us.

I am in awe of the fact that God has written His love letter
to the world in the hearts of ordinary people to be delivered to other ordinary
people. God didn't send a text message or social media post to the world. He
sent us. We are to carry His message and to make disciples.

I find this very telling of God since sending is such a part of who He is and what
He does.

Look up the following verses and answer the corresponding questions:

John 3:17; 17:23; 20:21. Who sent whom into the world? Why?

John 14:25-26; 16:7; Acts 2:1-13. Who sent whom? Where?

Matthew 28:18-20; Acts 13:1-3. Who sent whom? Where?

In all these verses you looked up, did you notice the progression of whom God sends and where He sends them? Note your observations.

Is God still sending people out today?

Imagine, then, if God sent us but we never arrived. What would happen?

When my letters to Mum never arrived, and I apologized and acknowledged that my letter must be lost, I never once said, "Mum, you must be lost," because Mum wasn't lost. My letter was.

In essence, we're living letters sent by God to a lost and broken world. But if we never arrive, then perhaps we are the ones who are lost. Could it be that even though Jesus has sent us, just like a letter, maybe, unknowingly, without intending to, we've become …

- Lost in our fears?
- Lost in our shame and guilt?
- Lost in our unforgiveness and condemnation?
- Lost in our offense and bitterness?
- Lost in our indifference and apathy?
- Lost in our religious practices and self-righteousness?
- Lost in our separation and segregation?
- Lost in our busyness and pursuit of comfort and safety?

- Lost in our competition and comparisons?
- Lost in our debates, tribes, or denominations?

As you read this list, did any of these ideas tug at your heart? Are you lost in any of these things? Or are there other things keeping people from hearing the gospel message written on your heart?

You are God's love letter to your world. If you realize you've been lost somewhere en route, then let me help you find your way home. Let me help you find your way back to your purpose. You are chosen to be sent. You are a letter to be read. You have a message to be shared.

Believe me when I say, Mum was never happier than when a letter that had been lost was found. She'd immediately open it and devour all the latest news about my girls. She'd even share it with her neighbors. Everyone was kept up to date on her granddaughters in California!

Imagine how much more meaningful, how much more valuable you and the message you have to share are to your world.

# DAY 3
## WE ARE A SPIRITUAL GPS

When Nick and I were first married, there were no iPhones with apps for navigating. We used maps or a map book—the kind that blocked the entire front window of the car when unfolded and for some reason could never be folded back into its original shape. The map book required you to look up a street name in the index at the back of the book, then flip to the page where the street should be, and then follow the letter from the top of the page to the corresponding number on the side of the page to locate the exact address of where you wanted to go.

When Nick drove and I navigated with these archaic tools, things got a little stressful. Our marriage was wonderfully blissful until we got in a car together.

When electronic GPS devices came along I felt so relieved, as though we'd been delivered from some kind of navigational marital bondage. I'm convinced that our marriage was saved by the Father, Son, Holy Spirit, and Navman! With one simple purchase, we experienced a peace we had never known.

But I quickly discovered that the marketing people got it all wrong. It was not a Navman, it was a Navwoman—the voice that came out of this device was a velvety smooth woman's voice. She would say things like, "At the roundabout, take the second exit," and when we missed the exit, she'd say in this breathy voice with slow pauses, "Rerouting … rerouting."

Initially, I thought she was great, and I named her Matilda. But there came a day when Matilda really started to get under my skin. I began to notice that Nick willingly obeyed everything she said! He didn't get irritated with her when she told him that he'd made a mistake and needed to make a U-turn. He didn't get grumpy or talk back. He silently complied. I was shocked. I gave the man two children, birthed from my own body, and he listened to this other woman more than he ever did to me!

Well, let me just say, I took care of Matilda. When I got in the car alone, I showed her who was the real woman in our family. When I'd start driving and she'd tell me to turn left or right in that buttery smooth voice, I'd say no, and I'd drive straight past the turn, just to show her a thing or two. I loved it when she got all confused and her screen would turn snowy white. I'd speed past the next exit, just to see if I could make her flatline. "That'll teach you," I'd say.

Needless to say, Matilda had a very short life span. One time I even said to Nick, "It's her or me. You choose." He chose wisely, and yet, I have to admit, despite my crazy reaction to a machine—albeit with a smooth, velvety, buttery voice—I can't deny that she was comforting at times. If we were lost, she knew how to get us back on track. If we were in an unfamiliar city, she knew how to help us navigate one-way streets, construction detours, and confusing freeways. Wherever we were, she knew how to point us in the right direction—no matter how badly we messed up.

*Lost is not a state God wants us or anyone else to remain in.*

Isn't that what God wants to do for those who are lost and have never found a relationship with Jesus Christ? Isn't that why we're sent as love letters to a lost and broken world? To help them get on track?

Lost is not a state God wants us or anyone else to remain in. Not physically or spiritually. Have you ever been separated from one of your kids in a store, at the mall, or at a theme park? Or seen a parent who has? *Frantic* is a word that comes to mind.

As much as parents are driven to find kids when they're lost, imagine how God feels toward us. Even though He knows—and we know—not everyone will choose Him, Jesus wants everyone found.

Read 1 Timothy 2:3-4 and 2 Peter 3:9. What is the heart of these passages?

Read Luke 19:10. What was Jesus' mission?

Jesus came to earth committed to going out of His way to reroute lost people.

How did you get to Jesus? Write a paragraph in the space provided below describing how you went from being lost to found. Think about all the ways God used people to reach you.

In order to be like a GPS and guide people to Jesus, I believe we need to understand how and why people are lost. There is no point in trying to redirect someone who is not looking for directions. I have always loved Luke 15 because it gives us a unique perspective on how people end up lost. Remember, when we change the lens through which we see people, we see them differently.

Let's walk through the stories in Luke 15 together and become what I call "lostologists"—people who are passionate experts at finding, understanding, and rerouting the lost. I know you won't find *lostologist* in any dictionary, and yes, I somewhat made it up, but I think it's a perfectly logical title to call ourselves.

Think about it. In the English language, the suffix "ology" is tacked on to numerous words to denote "the study of." For example, if you study the heart, you're a cardiologist. If you study humans, you're an anthropologist. If you study crime, you're a criminologist.

Are you catching on? So, why not call ourselves lostologists?

## Lost-ol-o-gist

1. People who are passionate experts at understanding the lost.

2. People who want to reach the lost.

(I couldn't resist highlighting this definition and making it official. I graduated from Sydney University with a B.A. in English, so perhaps part of my calling yet to unfold is to write a dictionary. When I do, I'll be sure to include *lostologist*!)

> Let's dive into our study on the lost. Look up Luke 15 and read the first seven verses, then write verse 7 in the space provided below.

I totally get these verses. Having grown up in Australia, with New Zealand just across the Tasman Sea, I understand a lot about sheep. New Zealand has more sheep than people. It's common to drive through the countryside and see hundreds of sheep in a pen but one little sheep in the distance on a hillside all by himself. He is so focused on eating that he has no idea how lost he is. He's preoccupied, head down, happily munching on the grass.

> Now read verses 8-10 and write verse 10 in the space provided below.

> Finish up the three stories by reading verses 11-32. In all three stories there is great rejoicing when what was lost was found. Write what three things were lost and then found.
> 1.
> 2.
> 3.

Like sheep, some people have wandered off. They're not bad or evil; they're often nice people preoccupied with life. They are part of the multitudes who are trying to pay the bills, deal with disappointment, navigate dating relation-ships, maintain friendships, keep their kids out of trouble, hold their marriages together, and hang onto their jobs. Of course, their sinfulness is what separates them from God. But their preoccupation with getting through another day has caused them to not realize they are lost. They don't mean to be lost. They didn't intend to get lost. But they are lost. They are separated from the Shepherd.

Whom do you know that fits this description?

While some people are preoccupied, others have been wounded. Someone has been careless with them, and they are lost. All we need to do is open up social media or a news app on our phones to see that there is so much pain, injustice, and suffering throughout the world. It's hard not to see how careless people can be with other people.

I come from a background of abandonment, adoption, and abuse, so I know how it feels to be impacted by others' actions. When I was lost—before I was found in Christ—I ended up far from God, in large part because of the pain I had suffered through others' carelessness. I was left full of shame, guilt, anger, and unforgiveness.

I know that it is our own sin that keeps us separated from God, but my experience has helped me to understand that some people who are far away from God have been deeply hurt and have confused people's carelessness for God's indifference. Could it be they're stuck because they've believed a lie of the enemy? Could it be they've given up on being found because they believe lost is all there is?

Do you know someone who has been carelessly treated? How has that carelessness contributed to his or her lostness?

Can you think of a time you have been careless with your words? Careless with your opinions? Careless with your social media posts? What about a time you were careless in choosing your friends?

God wants us to be mindful of why we are here on earth—to reroute people to Jesus, not make them want to run from Him. What we say and do—and how we say and do it—matters.

In Jesus' third parable in Luke 15, He described a son who walked away from his family. Perhaps this is the story that hits home more than any other because we all know someone who has walked away, someone who has miscalculated that life without the Father is better than life with the Father. Are we supposed to love even those who go off and squander everything? People from loving homes, stable situations, and church backgrounds? Yes. We absolutely are. Even when it's hard to do so.

Who in your life is most like the son who walked away?

Is it difficult for you to show this person love and compassion? Why or why not?

God doesn't want anyone to be lost. He is represented as the shepherd who sought the lost sheep. The woman who searched relentlessly for the coin. The father who ran to his son.

God is on a mission to seek and save the lost, and He has invited us to join Him in that mission.

God gave us a spiritual GPS system—not Matilda, but the Holy Spirit—to guide us to the lost, and to empower us so we can help them be found.

God almost always uses people to reroute other people. He sent Philip to the Ethiopian eunuch (Acts 8:26-39), Peter to Cornelius (Acts 10:1-33), and Paul to Lydia and the Philippian jailer (Acts 16:11-15,25-34).

Let's go help the lost find their way to Jesus, rerouting them through friendship, encouragement, a meal, a ride to work—whatever it is that meets them at their point of need.

Who is it that God is sending you to now?


How does God want to use you to help this person see Him?


Begin by praying daily for this person to come to Christ.

In the prayer below, fill in the name of the person God is sending you to. I can't wait to hear how someone who was lost is now found, and we can rejoice as heaven rejoices!

> I tell you, in the same way, there will be more joy in heaven over one sinner who repents than over ninety-nine righteous people who don't need repentance.
> LUKE 15:7

*Heavenly Father, You came to seek and to save the lost. I know it is Your desire for every person to come to know You and the depths of Your love. I lift _____ up to You and pray for them to be found in You. Use me, Lord, to help them be rerouted and give themselves to You, entrusting their heart fully to You. In Jesus' name I pray. Amen.*

# DAY 4

## WE ARE SALT AND LIGHT

Growing up Greek, it wasn't enough that we liberally salted food when we cooked it, we added even more when we ate it. Reaching for the saltshaker before even taking a bite was normal. What is it about salty food that makes us so happy?

Adding even a little salt can make a huge difference. And the alternatives just won't do.

> Read Matthew 5:13. Jesus called us the salt of the earth. Why would He compare us to a seasoning we put on our food?

> Read Matthew 5:14-15. What else did Jesus call us?

Why did Jesus call us salt and light? Maybe it's because salt and light are both agents of change. They are catalysts, meaning that by their very makeup they can't help but change what they come in contact with. Yet, they never change.

In the first century there was no refrigeration as we know it, so salt was used to preserve food. It's a method that worked so well we still preserve some food with salt in the modern day, like fish, bacon, and even a few vegetables. Since salt is a catalyst, even when we add it to food to season or preserve it, it never changes in composition—and it makes everything taste wonderful.

> Read Colossians 4:6. What did Paul say about salt? What did he mean?

Too many times I've had to go back to my husband or my children or someone on my team because what I said wasn't gracious. My words may have been right, but they weren't salted well.

When was the last time you spoke without seasoning your words? How was what you said received?

Jesus knew that a little bit of seasoning in what we say to a lost and dying world could make all the difference in someone receiving it.

In Matthew 5, Jesus also called us light. How is light a catalyst?

Consider what light does to the dark: dispels it. Illuminates it. Changes the environment so we can go from blindness to sight. Isn't that why we flip on the light as we enter a room? We don't want to stumble over the coffee table or a pair of shoes. We want the darkness to be eradicated so we can see.

Salt and light. Agents of change. Part of our identity as His disciples. Things He empowered us to be on the earth and in the lives of people.

Hopefully we'll embrace this identity and never underestimate our power to effect change in someone else's life. I underestimated this power once. I've never forgotten it and have made it a point to never make the same mistake.

While in college, I made a friend who appeared to have everything. She was beautiful, confident, and successful. She had good grades, achievements, opportunities, and wealth—everything I felt I didn't have. Over the months we grew close and often met on campus to eat lunch, study, or catch up on life.

So when she disappeared for three days straight, I was naturally alarmed. She didn't answer my calls, and I didn't see her anywhere on campus. I grew more and more concerned until the third day, when she surprisingly surfaced during lunch.

She told me that she had been to a nonstop party where most everyone had taken drugs to stay awake. I'll never forget what she said to me: "There was so much love. There was so much joy. There was so much peace that I was blown away." And with that, she put her hand in her pocket and pulled out this little flower. "I loved it so much, Chris, that I didn't want you to miss out on the experience, so I saved you half a tablet."

I kindly declined her offer, but I was rattled to my core. I was a fairly new Christian, but I couldn't help but think to myself, *This girl loves you so much that she didn't want you to miss out on the love and joy and peace from a drug. And you, Christine, have the Holy Spirit of God, the true source of love and joy and peace, living on the inside of you. Christine, you are too embarrassed to talk about God because you think she doesn't need Him, but the one thing she needs the most is God.*

Afterward, I found an empty room and wept. I made a promise to God that I would never allow anyone's passion about anything—drugs, money, success, or even a cause—to be more passionate than my love for Him and my willingness to go and tell people who He is and what He wants to give them—eternal life.

I was convinced my friend had it all, so much so that I reasoned she didn't need to hear the gospel, when the gospel was what she needed most from me.

Why do we easily recognize people with messed-up lives as lost, but fail to recognize that those who seem to have it all together are lost too? God wants us to understand that lost people look like all people.

Since that day, I have never forgotten there is a God-shaped vacuum in every human heart that only God can fill with the love, joy, and peace of Christ.

Read Matthew 5:16 and record Jesus' instruction.

Who in your world looks like they have everything? Do they have the most important thing—Jesus?

Read John 10:10. What kind of life did Jesus come to give us?

Our world today is extremely diverse. It's hard to go anywhere and not bump into someone who lives, cooks, dresses, or thinks differently than we do. Often we meet people who embrace ideas we find shocking, concerning, polarizing, or even offensive. But that can't stop us. Jesus has called, empowered, and equipped us to go into the world and help people move from lost to found.

Read John 17:14-19 and summarize what Jesus prayed for us.

Jesus wants us to be in the world but not of the world. We are salt and light sent into the world. We effect change but we don't change composition. We don't embrace the values of the world but we do embrace the people in the same way Jesus did.

*We don't embrace the values of the world, but we do embrace the people in the same way Jesus did.*

Jesus loved the poor, the ostracized, the oppressed, and the dispossessed. He included those marginalized by society, those considered to have no value. Everywhere He went, He broke down barriers and built bridges between people and God.

Who do you think would fit into these categories of people today?

Jesus constantly bumped into people who didn't share His viewpoints or His values, but that didn't deter Him from His purpose ... the same purpose He's assigned to us—to seek and save the lost. That's our purpose too.

If we are to fulfill our purpose, we need to go where the lost are. We can't go and make disciples while keeping the world at arm's length. We can't make following Jesus fundamentally about behavior modification. Christianity is not about behavior modification; it's about Jesus. Jesus did not come to make bad people good, but to make dead people alive. Jesus wants us to go and make disciples. If we avoid the world by staying instead of going because the world acts like the world, then how will we bring salt and light to it?

As people who are found and sent to find the lost, we can stand separate from the effects of sin while fully embracing people who are wounded, hurting, and defiled by sin. I didn't have to go to a party with my friend or accept the pill she offered me, but what I realized is that I needed to be salt and light in her world. I needed to love her, to tell her about Jesus, and to show her His indescribable love for her.

There was nothing for me to fear—no worldliness for me to run from—because we are to be in the world to change it and not be fearful of it changing us.

Read 1 John 4:4 and write what is promised to us.

We can't be the salt of the earth if we don't get out of the saltshaker—if we don't get out of our comfort zones and intentionally mingle among the worldly. They are the ones who are lost and need to be found. They are the ones who are going in the wrong direction and need to be rerouted.

As you reflect on all we've covered today, what steps do you believe God is calling you to take to get out of the saltshaker and into the world? Be specific. Whom is He calling you to invest in?

Jesus chose you and has sent you to carry His message into the world. How has your approach to His mission changed since beginning this week of study?

# DAY 5

## *WE ARE WORKERS*

God has chosen you and me to make Him known in this world. There is no plan B. We are God's plan A. He is aware of our flaws, potential fears, doubts, and insecurities. He understands we may feel completely inadequate. How can our minds not be flooded with a myriad of questions? How can we not break out in a cold sweat when we think about what going into all the world might mean? Still, none of this is a surprise to God, and not one of our limitations daunts Him. He knows all the people He wants us to reach. He sees them just as clearly as He sees us.

In John 4:35, Jesus said, "Listen to what I'm telling you: Open your eyes and look at the fields, because they are ready for harvest."

What is the ready harvest Jesus is talking about?

In my efforts to fully understand the harvest, I turned to my friend and bestselling author, Ann Voskamp, who describes herself as a farmer's wife and mama to seven. She and her husband manage a farm of more than seven hundred acres, where they grow corn, soybeans, and wheat. As a city girl who knows nothing about farming, I asked Ann to teach me everything she knows about harvest, especially what she and her husband do during harvesttime.

## har·vest

1. the process or period of gathering in crops.
synonyms: harvesting, reaping, picking, collecting[19]

Ann started by explaining that where they live is subject to heavy rains and evening blankets of dew. So, close to harvesttime, her husband constantly checks to see if the wheat is dry enough to harvest. And the moment the wheat is ready, he begins.

He may rise at 2:00 or 3:00 a.m. to care for their livestock so he can get into the fields around 4:00 or 5:00 a.m.—and then he doesn't stop. He doesn't stop to eat. He doesn't stop to empty the combine harvester. Everyone works together so he can keep driving the combine and harvesting the wheat. Ann prepares meals he can eat with one hand and takes them to him in the field. Others driving tractors pulling auger wagons drive alongside him so the wheat can be transferred from his bin to their wagons without him ever having to stop. During the most recent corn harvest, he drove the combine all night long because the break in the weather was a narrow window of time. Of course, if he works all night, then everyone else works all night too.

Listening to Ann, I realized the harvesting of each kind of crop is preceded by months of preparation and work that may seem invisible because it's behind the scenes—like repairing and maintaining machinery and catching up on paper-work. Private preparation leads to short windows of public harvesting.

How is this principle true in our spiritual lives? How is God using this study to prepare you for harvest?

Ann said that when it's harvesttime, everything else gets put aside, including extracurricular activities, dinners with friends, community events, and sports for the kids. Everyone's focus turns to the harvest.

Not being a farmer like Ann's husband, I don't live through seasons of harvesting crops; still, God wants me to keep the harvest on my mind.

Through the years, I've made changes to simplify my life so I could focus more on the harvest. I've made simple changes and life-altering ones. For example, I've missed fun events with friends because I knew my time was better spent with someone far from God who needed a little light in the darkness. My family also moved to the United States from Sydney to shave fourteen hours off our commute, allowing us to spend more time among the harvest in the U.S. and in the countries where the work of A21 continues to expand. To this day, I am con-stantly tweaking and simplifying things in my life so I can stay focused on the harvest.

What is one way you can simplify your life so you can better focus on the harvest?

How can you influence others around you (family, small group, volunteer team) to do the same? Be specific.

Ann said that every day of every week in the months preparing for harvest, her husband watches the weather, looking to the sky and paying attention to the forecast. Based on the weather, he adjusts what he will do that night, the next morning, and the next afternoon. It's a perpetual state of watchfulness, of constant readiness. He once said he felt like a fireman who is always alert. And when the alarm sounds, when the harvest is ready, nothing else matters.

God wants us to live with this same watchfulness, to look for the lost people around us. We're to pray for them, encourage them, and watch for ways we can help reroute them.

Ann said whether her husband is harvesting beans, getting ready to plant wheat, or researching next year's corn yields, harvest is always on his mind. In every decision he makes, every step he takes, he thinks about the harvest. He's always learning, always growing, always preparing for harvest. Ever watchful. Ever aware. Because in his mind, it's always harvesttime.

God wants us to think about the harvest the same way Ann's husband does. Always ready for the harvest. Always sensitive to the leading of the Holy Spirit to know who He's pointing out to us.

How can you grow in that kind of readiness?

What was Jesus' command in John 4:35? Open your eyes and look at the fields! He wants our eyes wide open so we can see the people in our field of vision.

## field of vi·sion

1.  the entire area that a person is able to see when their eyes are fixed in one position.[20]

Do you realize we've been in the season of harvest for over two thousand years? Ever since Jesus walked the earth and brought the gift of salvation there have been souls ripe for the harvest, fields full of people waiting for us to come find them. What would happen if we started seeing our homes, schools, communities, and even shopping malls as fields ready for harvest?

Jesus spoke about the abundant harvest in Matthew 9:35-38. Read this passage and answer the following questions.

Whom would you describe in your sphere of influence as the harvest?

Whom would you describe as the workers?

Jesus said the harvest is _____. But the workers are _____.

Jesus didn't say there was a lack of work, only a lack of workers. Can you see that in our world today?

- There is no lack of need.
- There is no lack of people.
- There is no lack of causes.
- There is no lack of information.
- There is no lack of knowledge.
- There is no lack of opportunity.
- There is no lack of access to the Bible.
- There is no lack of Christian media.
- There is no lack of Christian books.
- There is no lack of good churches.
- There is no lack of access to Christian resources.

There's just a lack of workers.

## work·er

1. A person who does a specified type of work or who works in a specified way.[21]

Imagine if all Ann's children, extended family, and farm employees didn't help bring in the harvest, didn't want to be interrupted to do the work. What would happen?

Ann's sister has often said to her, "I don't know how you can be married to a farmer, because I can't count on you for anything. Everything I ask you to do, you say, 'Well it depends on the weather.'" That's because it does, literally! Ann and her family make plans, but they live with open minds, always flexible, always willing to interrupt their plans for the harvest.

Jesus was always willing to be interrupted. Always willing to see the one and bring in the harvest.

Based on Matthew 9:38, what was Jesus' solution to getting more workers?

Many people pray the Lord's Prayer (Matt. 6:9-13; Luke 11:2-4), but I suspect far fewer pray as Jesus instructed in Matthew 9:38. Why do you think that might be? Are you hesitant to pray that prayer? If so, why?

Harvesttime is an urgent time. What if we prayed a prayer like the one in Matthew 9:38 every day for the rest of this study?

*Lord of the harvest, I know the harvest is plentiful and the workers are few, so send me, Lord. Help me to look and to see—to see the broken and the lost. Help me to feel compassion and courage to reach out and pull someone close today. In Jesus' name I pray. Amen.*

What if we not only make Jesus' last command our biggest priority but also make His prayer our greatest priority as well? What if we pray together for workers to bring in the harvest?

Of course, don't be surprised if we're the workers God sends first. If the fields are ripe, how can we not be the answer to Jesus' prayer?

> Read 1 Corinthians 3:6-9. How does this passage apply to the work of the harvest? What roles are listed in these verses?

When it comes to the spiritual harvest, some sow, some water, and some reap. But God is the One who brings the growth. It's all a work of God, but He lets us enjoy the bounty.

I've thought a lot about what Ann taught me, especially concerning her husband's vigilant posture of watchfulness. He prepares, plants, grows, and harvests, but in every minute of every day of every cycle, he looks up. He looks to the heavens. He is expectant. He is diligent to control all he can, yet he knows he's dependent on the sovereignty of God for the harvest.

I love what Ann told me they do once the harvest is in: they enjoy a big meal where everyone laughs, lets off steam, and relaxes. They've handled the harvest with great care, and when it's done, they rest and celebrate.

You may be a city girl like me, and we may not understand one single thing about farming, but I bet we all know about celebrating. When I think of celebrating, I can't help but think of the parables we looked at yesterday from Luke 15. Peruse that chapter and note what happened with the return of the sheep, the coin, and the son.

Celebration! And what happens when one sinner repents and comes home? A huge party breaks out in heaven! Wow!

I don't know who is in your future that you're going to celebrate, but I believe there is someone. It's harvest season! And harvest season is the best season! Someone is out there in a field, ready, waiting for you.

God has seen you and chosen you so He can send you. All you have to do is go.

WEEK 3

# ILLUMINATE AND ELIMINATE YOUR BLIND SPOTS

## *REFRAME YOUR VIEW*

### WATCH
Watch Video Week 3, *It's Up to You,* and record your personal thoughts as you listen.

_____

_____

_____

_____

_____

_____

_____

_____

_____

_____

_____

_____

_____

_____

_____

_____

_____

_____

## DISCUSS

"Do you want to be healed?" (John 5:6, ESV). It's the question Jesus asked the man lying by the pool of Bethesda, and it's the question He's asking us today. I have found that there is always more in every area of our lives—more healing, more wholeness, more intimacy with Jesus, and more effectiveness for Jesus. There is always more transformation, more sanctification, and more freedom. Sometimes, embracing this "more" means going deep and cutting some things out. Other times, embracing more is akin to examining scar tissue or finding a bruise that needs tending. But no matter the depth of our wounds, God's promise to us stands: "He heals the brokenhearted and bandages their wounds" (Ps. 147:3).

> Pause for a moment. Look over your notes. What stood out to you from the video teaching?
>
> Are you prone to define yourself by your most prominent issue or by your identity in Christ? Explain.
>
> Why are we sometimes quick to identify people by their issues?
>
> Why do you think Jesus asked the man who'd been an invalid for thirty-eight years if he wanted to get well? Wouldn't that be obvious?
>
> If Jesus asked you if you wanted to be healed, what kind of answer would you give Him? Is asking for healing a struggle, or is it easy?
>
> What excuses do we give that keep us from healing and wholeness in Christ?
>
> Why is it that when we're broken and hurting we'll look everywhere else for help before turning to Christ? Has that been your experience?
>
> Why are healing and wholeness tied so closely to our ability to reach and minister to others?
>
> How have you experienced healing from Christ in the past? How has that healing impacted the people in your sphere of influence?

The invalid man was lying by a pool called Bethesda—a name that literally means "House of Mercy" or "House of Grace."[22] When Jesus healed the man, He ministered to him both mercy and grace. When Jesus heals us, He extends the same mercy and grace, and He wants us to receive it with open arms. He wants to help us get to the place where—in every area of our lives and hearts— we come to realize that what God has done *for* us is bigger than what others have done *to* us. That what God has said about us is greater than what others have said about us.

Do you want to be healed? It's a question Jesus asks over and over again throughout our lives, and He always wants our answer to be yes![23]

### MOVE

In what area of your life is Jesus asking you to get up, take your mat, and walk?

What steps will you take to do that?

### PRAY

Yes, Lord! I want to be healed! Please show me any areas in

my heart, soul, and mind that need Your healing. I want to be

free and to continue to bear fruit, the kind of fruit that remains.

# DAY 1
## *EXPAND YOUR PERIPHERAL VISION*

When Nick and I first began to teach Catherine about driving, we started by teaching her about the car itself and everything we do before we move the car even an inch. These are steps Nick and I have executed automatically for decades, steps like:

- adjusting the seat to comfortably reach the accelerator and brake;
- buckling the seat belt before even thinking about turning on the ignition;
- setting the mirrors to have the maximum view through the rearview window and out either side of the car in order to eliminate the blind spots.

A blind spot is an area in our range of vision we cannot see but we need to see. It's where our vision is obstructed but we don't know it's obstructed. When we're driving a car, it's the area just behind our shoulders. How many times have we experienced near misses because someone was riding in our blind spot?

### blind spot
1. the point of entry of the optic nerve on the retina, insensitive to light.

2. an area where a person's view is obstructed.[24]

I've read that you can eliminate blind spots by setting your rearview mirror to where you can see straight out the back, and then extending your side mirrors out fifteen degrees. If you do, the side mirrors become extensions of your rearview mirror. With all three mirrors set properly, you will extend your view and have full coverage of everything behind you and on both sides.[25]

Isn't that how God wants us to see? To have wide-sweeping, peripheral vision with no spiritual blind spots?

When we can't see where we need to see, we have a blind spot that needs to be illuminated so it can be eliminated.

In a car, we have three mirrors to help us eliminate blind spots. In life, we have the Word of God that acts like a mirror.

Read James 1:22-25. Describe how God's Word acts like a mirror for our reflection and growth.

When we look into the mirror of God's Word, it shows us who God made us to be—His image bearers. It shows us how we're to live in order to thrive and flourish. It shows us where we need to make adjustments in our lives. God uses His Word to illuminate our blind spots so we can eliminate them.

*God's Word shows us who God made us to be—His image bearers.*

So often our blind spots develop without us even realizing it, and they remain obscured outside our peripheral vision as prejudices, preconceptions, thoughts, feelings, judgments, culture, or traditions. Sometimes our success or gifting leads to pride, arrogance, or self-reliance—common blind spots that are easy to miss. Sometimes it's the pain, trauma, or hurts we've endured that create blind spots.

What are some other common blind spots? How can they develop?

Describe a blind spot you had that was illuminated and then eliminated.

The Pharisees and Sadducees were two groups of religious leaders who had blind spots. They often sought to trap Jesus by questioning Him. In answering their questions, Jesus illuminated their blind spots. But they were so concerned with dotting every "i" and crossing every "t" they couldn't see them.

In Matthew 22, the religious leaders asked Jesus three questions. Read the following passages and note what they asked Jesus and how He answered them.

| PASSAGE | QUESTION | ANSWER |
|---|---|---|
| Matthew 22:15-22 | | |
| Matthew 22:23-33 | | |
| Matthew 22:34-40 | | |

Let's focus on the last and perhaps toughest question they asked Jesus: "Teacher, which command in the law is the greatest?" (v. 36). Jesus answered with what He called the two greatest commandments. Write them here.

1.

2.

Jesus said the second command is like the first. We'll dive into why this is so important, but first, let's focus on how both commandments reveal how we love God, how we love others, and how we love ourselves.

To love God with all our hearts, all our souls, and all our minds is to express the totality and the comprehensiveness of our love for Him. It's to love God with all our being. It's the greatest and most important command—and out of it flows the second that is like it: to love our neighbor as ourselves.

What is the connection between these two commandments? How is one dependent on the other?

Based on the two greatest commandments, we need to see ourselves the way God does in order to see our neighbors the way God does. We need to love ourselves so that we can properly love our neighbor as ourselves.

I felt a twinge just then, didn't you? Why is it that loving ourselves makes us feel so uncomfortable? Aren't we supposed to deny ourselves? Prefer others over ourselves? Is it even Christian to love ourselves? Yes, because God said to.

Can we love our neighbors the way God wants us to if we have blind spots? Explain.

When Nick and I were engaged, he jokingly told me he had one goal in life: "I want to love you as much as you do."

Trust me, the fact that I loved myself at all at that point was nothing short of a miracle, because I had spent so many years ashamed of myself. My shame was caused by a number of factors, including being abandoned at birth and adopted two weeks later, and then being abused for many years of my childhood. The fact that I had reached a place where I could let Jesus do a work in me—to the point that I not only liked myself, but was also beginning to flourish in life and even love myself—was a testimony to God's goodness, power, and unending love for me.

Yes, I still have plenty of blind spots, but I am no longer afraid of the process of allowing the Holy Spirit to illuminate them through the Word. In fact, I invite Him daily to do a work in me, and I welcome the changes He makes, because they enable me to walk in greater freedom and to reach and serve more people. God wants to do more in us, so He can do more through us, so more people can be reached. But for that to happen we have to engage in His process.

Wouldn't it be more comfortable if Christianity were about loving God only? With all our hearts, souls, and minds? Yes, it would. But we're to love Him first, and then out of that love, we're to love others as we love ourselves. This is what

He's instructed us to do. He wants us to remember how valuable we are and how valuable everyone else is.

When I was growing up, Mum never let us use the good crystal glasses she and Dad received as wedding presents, because we were saving them for when the "special people" came to visit. I lived at home until I married at thirty, and we never used those crystal glasses. I tell my daughters, "*We* are the special people! Get it all out. Set the table with the best crystal and silverware. And if a glass breaks, we'll go buy some fabulous plastic ones! Problem solved!" I don't want my daughters to think guests are more worthy or special than they are.

I understand we live in a self-absorbed world, and as Christian women we strive to never be focused on ourselves, but what if, in our efforts to not be self-focused, we've simply forgotten ourselves? Overlooked ourselves? Even ignored ourselves? Could that be an indicator of a blind spot? And is that blind spot preventing us from seeing others and making them feel seen?

How might you be ignoring yourself right now?


What are some of the consequences of overlooking yourself?


Nowhere in the Word does it say we are to forget about ourselves. It does say we are to deny ourselves (Matt. 16:24), but that speaks to denying our flesh, our desires, our agendas ... not our well-being.

God wants us to know we are His chosen daughters. He wants to take care of us, and He wants us to take care of us, because blind spots can form in any area of our lives without us realizing it. And those blind spots can interfere with loving our neighbor as ourselves.

Walking Catherine through how to eliminate her blind spots while driving got me thinking about how important it is to allow God to illuminate and eliminate our blind spots spiritually—those places in our lives that stop us from being able to see the person God has put in our path. He wants to heal the broken places in our hearts, souls, and minds that keep us from being able to love Him, love others, and love ourselves the way He wants us to.

Just like we can move the side mirrors on our car a mere fifteen degrees to eliminate blind spots, I believe we can make similar incremental adjustments spiritually. A few degrees here, a few degrees there. Imagine if that's all it took for an area of our hearts to be healed so we could see what we couldn't see before and love more than we've ever loved before.

That's where we'll start tomorrow.

# DAY 2
## GOD WANTS TO HEAL YOUR HEART

If I ever need a backup career, I could become an airline attendant. For the past twenty-five years, I've flown more than most pilots. I'm healthy. I'm cheerful. I like serving others. (See, I'm already working on my interview answers!) And I already know how to recite all the safety instructions—from the seat belt demonstration to how to put on your life vest and inflate it. I can even instruct you in how to use your oxygen mask:

> If necessary due to a change in cabin pressure, an oxygen mask will drop from the panel above your seat. Place the mask over your nose and mouth and breathe normally. ... Remember to fix your own mask before helping others.[26]

That last line always gets my attention.

It's the most counterintuitive instruction to our Christian hearts and minds. We have been taught so well to put others first, to not be self-centered, to prefer one another over ourselves, that we've lost sight of the importance of self-care.[27]

Jesus said, "Love your neighbor as yourself" (Matt. 22:39). How can we love our neighbor if we don't love ourselves? And if we dare decide to love ourselves, where do we begin?

Well, since Jesus said to love God with all our hearts, souls, and minds, and *then* to love our neighbor as ourselves, I suggest we start with His first instruction—to love Him.

Every year I get a physical from head to toe, and one organ the doctor always checks is my heart. To examine it, the nurses and technicians start with the least invasive test—an electrocardiogram. They attach those little electrodes to my chest, get me on the treadmill, and check to see if my heart is beating rhythmically. Next comes the echocardiogram, where they take an ultrasound to examine the heart chambers, even measuring the flow of blood into and out of each one.

My doctor knows that a strong heart with clear arteries is vital to my overall health. So she reminds me yearly to exercise regularly, eat a healthy diet, and do everything I can to maintain heart health.

I believe our spiritual hearts need the same kind of regular checkups. Life can throw us curveballs that cause devastating heartbreak, and heartbreak can lead to a spiritual heart attack.

Maybe your heart was broken when you were …

- shamed publicly by a boss;
- overlooked for a promotion;
- taken for granted;
- derailed and unable to finish school;
- rejected by your own parent;
- wrongly accused by one of your children;
- betrayed by a best friend;
- shocked at losing a loved one way too early;
- released unexpectedly from a job;
- exposed for not living up to your own standards;
- devastated by a divorce;
- ruined financially and left to start over.

Describe a time when your heart was broken.

Did your heartbreak cause you to pull back from others? Did it adversely affect your willingness to love and to trust? Explain.

Once we've been hurt deeply, we're tempted to keep people at arm's length. We're hesitant to trust, care, and minister. The Message translation of

Psalm 34:18 says, "If your heart is broken, you'll find GOD right there; if you're kicked in the gut, he'll help you catch your breath." Someone has to be close to kick you in the gut, right? God wants us to invite Him in to heal our hearts.

Look up Psalm 147:3, and note God's promises to the brokenhearted.

God is not callous to our pain. He promises His presence and tender healing. But God wants us to protect our spiritual heart as much as our physical one.

Read Proverbs 4:23. What are we to do and why?

Our hearts are the source of our very lives—spiritually and physically. Physically, our ability to live stems from the condition of our hearts. Spiritually, our ability to love stems from the condition of our hearts. How vital, then, that we guard them.

Read the following passages and note the importance of our hearts:

1 Samuel 16:7

Matthew 6:19-21

Matthew 12:33-34

Romans 10:9-10

It's no wonder Jesus began the greatest commandment in Matthew 22:37 with, "Love the Lord your God with all your heart ..." God tells us to guard our hearts because therein lies the seat of our passion. Our hearts are what drive us and compel us. They're the essence of our character, and the place from which we love passionately. And when we are passionate about something, we are all in, whether that's loving God, our family, or the lost.

When Nick and I first met, he launched a full-scale passionate pursuit to capture my heart. We met in a class I was covering for a colleague at our church's Bible college. Nick was a student on the front row. As he likes to say, "I fell in love with the teacher."

Not long after that class, Nick started showing up at the pool where I swam at 6:00 a.m. He swam in the lane next to me for weeks. I later learned he'd never, ever swam laps, and certainly not at 6:00 a.m. Once we married, he never swam laps again! Passion drove him to get up and be at that pool, all in hopes of winning my heart.

If God wants us to love Him with all our hearts, then our hearts must have the capacity to do so; but oftentimes, life's heartaches steal our passion.

When we're disappointed, disillusioned, or discouraged, it's easy to grow numb, angry, unforgiving, offended, bitter, or resentful. Our passion wanes and we ose heart.

Think of how many times you've heard someone say, "Well, her heart just isn't in it." Isn't that what happens when our hearts are broken? Isn't that how our hearts leave someplace long before we do?

- Can't we be in a marriage, but our heart not be in it?
- Can't we be in a church, but our heart not be in it?
- Can't we be on a sports team, but our heart not be in it?
- Can't we have a great job, but our heart not be in it?
- Can't we be in a friendship, but our heart not be in it?

Is there an area where you're functioning but you recognize that your heart just isn't in it?

As Christians, we often intellectually embrace the Great Commission (Matt. 28:19-20). We know we should search for the lost until they are found. We want to love God with all our hearts, souls, and minds, and we want to love our neighbors as ourselves. But we get hurt. We grow weary. We get overwhelmed. And we find ourselves with broken hearts.

Read the following passages and note the actions we are to take, the truths we are to remember, and the promises we are to claim to find healing and rest for our battered hearts.

**Psalm 23**

**Psalm 61:1-2**

**Isaiah 40:29-31**

**Matthew 11:28**

**John 16:33**

**Galatians 6:9**

**Philippians 4:6-7**

**1 Peter 5:7**

God wants us to love Him with all our hearts, souls, and minds, but to do that we need to invite Him in to transform us so we can then love our neighbor as ourselves. We need to go inward so we can go outward.

We'll continue this journey of healing tomorrow as we invite God in to heal our souls.

# DAY 3

## *WHEN YOUR SOUL HAS A BLIND SPOT*

While I was writing this Bible study, Nick was training for one of the world's most athletically challenging mountain bike races. He started training one year out, but on his second day riding and jumping the hills near our house, he flew headfirst over the front of his bike. Somewhere on the way to his near perfect landing, he cut his leg open.

When he came hobbling in the front door, it took all the strength I had to get past the blood and examine his wound. We cleaned it up, coated it with anti-biotic ointment, bandaged it, and tended to it for several days. We kept watch for any signs of infection. Though he tried to walk normally, most of the time he limped around or hopped on one foot. He was careful not to put too much weight on his leg so the wound wouldn't reopen.

I find it interesting that wounds—like Nick's—are so visible even when we attempt to cover them up and go on with life like they aren't there.

But breaking an arm or a leg, that's quite different. A bone break is usually just an internal wound. We can see evidence of it perhaps because of a dangling limb or swelling in and around the break. We can feel it because of pain or soreness. But we can't see what's hidden under our skin.

When I snapped my ACL, tore my MCL, and fractured my right knee in a skiing accident years ago, though nothing looked out of place on the outside, the pop, pop, pop sound I heard when it happened—and the pain I immediately felt—told me something was wrong on the inside. The doctor at the hospital had a pretty good idea of what injuries I had sustained, but like any good practitioner he ordered an MRI so he could see what wasn't visible on the surface.

So it is with our broken hearts. Despite the pain, most people we encounter on any given day have no idea we're walking around with an unbearable ache. We go on with life—work, family, church, even parties—and expertly hide our broken hearts. But a spiritual wound is much harder to hide. Though we clean it, coat it, and bandage it, if we don't administer proper wound care until it's healed, it will leak through at some point for all to see. Left unattended, the wound will grow infected and seep into every part of our lives, adversely affecting our ability to feel seen, chosen, and sent—and our ability to help others feel seen, chosen, and sent.

> Have you ever been in a situation where a wound you thought was healed suddenly got exposed? And all the old feelings associated with it came rushing back? Describe the experience.

I remember when a wound I thought I had bandaged quite well burst wide open. I was in my twenties and leading a nationwide youth ministry with a team who was passionate about reaching young people. Back then—not wanting to disappoint God and finding way too much of my significance and security in what I did—I overcommitted myself on a routine basis. I had no awareness of how my driven life and leadership impacted my team. Each one of them was faithful and passionate, so I kept pushing harder.

While I was under the illusion that everything was humming along wonderfully, my team was growing more and more exhausted. That's when Joanna, someone I depended on immensely, resigned. She painted a picture of what it was really like to work under my leadership. She was incredibly kind, but she described how I set unrealistic deadlines, pushed for impossible performance standards, and was impatient to achieve results because nothing was ever enough.

Because of wounds in my soul I had bandaged but hadn't let God heal, I took her comments very personally. All I could hear in my head were my self-imposed judgments: *bad leader, critical leader, demanding leader, perfectionist.* I felt rejected, and a lifetime of self-defense mechanisms sprang into action without me even recognizing them.

In the days and weeks that followed, I went to God in a way I never had before. I asked Him to heal all the places in my soul I didn't want to acknowledge or think about. I could no longer run from the reality that wounded areas of my soul were wounding others. And I suspect we all have wounded places in our souls.

What places in your soul have you covered over that need proper wound care?

God said to love Him with all our hearts and our souls so we can love our neighbor as ourselves. God wants to heal our souls so we can do as He's asked.

Look up 3 John 2. What did John pray for his friend Gaius?

**ZOOM IN**
The Greek word for prosper is *euodoo* and means "to succeed," "to have things go well," or "to enjoy favorable circumstances."[28]

John was praying that his friend's physical health would match the level of his spiritual health, that his body would prosper as his soul prospered.

How does your soul's prospering affect other areas of your life?

And what about the opposite? How does your soul's sorrow affect you?

Our wounds can be exposed as fear, insecurity, shame, rejection, frustration, or anger. Wounds can originate from loss, abuse, or rejection. They can move us to isolate ourselves and lose ourselves, even to the point of depression. They can lead us to drive relentlessly or to give up. God wants to care for our wounds and heal them. He wants to transform us from the inside out so we can move forward and reach out to others.

When I was wounded, I leaked toxicity. It came out in my words, my attitudes, and my responses to people and situations. It affected my relationships at home, at work, and among my friends. My toxicity felt like something I couldn't control, and it would spill out when I least expected it. I reacted in situations—silently, verbally, emotionally.

List the last three times your soul was wounded and how you reacted.

1.

2.

3.

The wounds you listed are just the sort God wants to heal. He knows the impact wounds can have on our souls, but our hope and healing are always found in Him.

Read the following psalms. Note the psalmists' wounds but also their hope.

**Psalm 42**

**Psalm 63**

**Psalm 64**

In order for us to receive God's healing power, Christ has to dwell in us. Read Ephesians 3:17-19. What else do we need to be rooted in so we can receive God's healing?

Being rooted and grounded in God's love means believing in His love for us. Doesn't this go back to loving God with all our hearts, souls, and minds, and then out of that love, loving ourselves and our neighbors as ourselves? How comforting to know that God loves us—that He is for us!

Read Romans 8:28. Write God's promise below.

Before God began to heal my soul, it was hard to trust Him. I had been wounded at the hands of multiple abusers throughout my childhood, so it was hard to comprehend that He loved me. But when I began to understand that He is good, that He does good, and that He is working all things together for my good—even though things happened to me that weren't good—I accepted His healing work. When I was convinced of His love, I grew in my trust of Him.

I began to realize that Christ died for me while I was yet a sinner (Rom. 5:8), so why not invite Him in while I am yet unhealed in some areas?

All through the years, I have continued to trust Him from one level to the next. Yes, there were times when I thought He was disappointed in me, because I was disappointed in myself. There were times when I thought He was mad at me, because I was mad at myself. But eventually, as He engraved the redemptive truths in His Word deeper and deeper into my heart, I learned that He wasn't. He couldn't be because of what Christ accomplished on our behalf on the cross. As Paul declares so beautifully and definitively, "He made the one who did not know sin to be sin for us, so that in him we might become the righteousness of God" (2 Cor. 5:21). The bottom line is, God is love and He loves me (1 John 4:7-8).

God wants us to find healing and rest for our souls. Let's wrap up today's personal study by looking up two final verses that speak to finding God's rest. What comfort and encouragement do you find in these verses?

**Jeremiah 6:16**

**Matthew 11:28-30**

To love God with all our hearts, souls, and minds, and to love ourselves and our neighbor as ourselves, begins with letting God heal our broken hearts, our wounded souls, and our tormented minds. We'll deal with our minds tomorrow, but for now, let's pray together and ask God to heal our souls.

*Heavenly Father, You are the Great Physician. You have promised to heal my broken heart and bind up my wounds, so I give my wounds to You to clean and heal. Thank You for doing a healing work in me. I truly want to love You with all my heart, soul, and mind. Thank You for helping me live out Your commands. I love You. In Jesus' name I pray. Amen.*

# DAY 4

## *LOVE GOD WITH ALL YOUR MIND*

When I was a university student, I caught the train every morning at 7:30 from Seven Hills station in the western suburbs of Sydney where I lived to Redfern station in the center of Sydney where my school campus was located. The commute took forty-five minutes, and I was grateful for that time as I normally used the commute to catch up on my assignments. One particular morning, I was running late and had a lot on my mind because of an important exam that day. When I got to the top of the stairs leading to the various platforms, I skipped one habitual step: checking the destination board for delays or platform changes. I heard a train pull up to platform 4, and I immediately rushed down the stairs and jumped on board as the doors closed. *Just made it,* I thought.

As the train pulled out of the station, I noticed it wasn't headed toward downtown Sydney. In fact, it was going in the exact opposite direction—toward the mountains. I started to panic as the train picked up speed and an announcement came over the loudspeaker telling us to enjoy the ride on the express train to Katoomba, the beautiful Blue Mountains. I felt sick as I realized I couldn't get off the train. I was going to miss my exam, and I had no idea when there would be another train scheduled to take me back to where I started.

When the train stopped and the doors opened, I numbly stepped onto the platform and moaned aloud, "How did I get here?"

The stationmaster happened to be standing nearby. He looked at me with a grin and said, "Well, love, you got on the wrong train, didn't you?"

It was that simple. I had gotten on the wrong train and ended up in the wrong place.

How many times have you ended your day wondering, *God, how did I get here?* Not physically, but mentally and emotionally. You're angry again. Lonely again. Disillusioned again. Heartbroken again. Anxious again. Defeated again. Fearful again. Insecure again. Comparing again.

I sometimes imagine that God wants to say, "Well, love, you just got on the wrong train of thought, didn't you?"

Our thoughts, like a train, take us somewhere. I've discovered that if I don't manage where I want my thoughts to take me on a daily basis, I'll end up jumping on any train of thought, often ending up where I don't want to be.[29]

The good news is I can choose where I want to be!

God commanded us to love Him with our hearts, souls, and minds. And we want to. But if we are consumed with runaway thoughts, we can feel like we have a tormented mind—and that is the mind God wants to heal.

*Our thoughts, like a train, take us somewhere.*

We don't have to be held captive by thoughts that torment us and spiral out of control. God has given us the power to choose what we think.

Read Colossians 3:2. Write the verse in the space provided below and circle the first three words.

If Paul told the Colossians they could set their minds, we have the capacity to do the same.

When I was younger and didn't know how to cope with all the thoughts swirling in my head, I found ways to numb my pain. I buried myself in my work. I ignored situations, acting like I didn't care. I did care, of course, but I didn't know how to control what I thought about, which affected how I felt and how I responded. So I tried to escape mentally and emotionally from my own thoughts.

What about you? How do you try to escape from your own thoughts? Binge-watching TV? Social media? Shopping? A busy schedule?

Imagine how much anxiety would disappear from our lives if we learned how to set our minds at the start of every day instead of letting them jump on a train of thought and build speed throughout the day. And yet, I get it. Sometimes we have to start with resetting our minds every second, then every minute, building up to every hour! We have to find Scriptures that speak to what we're worrying over and speak those in prayer until the hope in those verses dominates our thoughts. When I'm renewing my mind in an area, I even write verses down. I write them on sticky notes and post them everywhere I can see them to remind myself of the truth.

Learning how to set our minds is the first step in getting control of our runaway thoughts. And what we set our minds on matters.

> Look back at Colossians 3:2. What are we to set our minds on? What does that mean?

Setting our minds on things above means keeping our minds focused on God, His Word, His ways, and His purposes. To do that requires a renewed mind.

> Read Romans 12:1-2. What was Paul's instruction in verse 2?

The key to being transformed—to learning how to set our minds—begins with renewing our minds. And that renewing takes place through the power of God and His Word. The psalmist said, "I have treasured your word in my heart so that I may not sin against you" (Ps. 119:11). A renewed mind is a mind filled with God's Word.[30] Only with a renewed mind can we manage our thoughts, change our mental default settings, and stop destructive patterns of thinking.

How many times have we changed our behaviors, our routines, even our eating habits only to slide right back into our old ways? The key to lasting change—to being transformed from the inside out—is to allow God to heal our hearts and souls and to renew our minds.

Paul said that when we receive Christ we are completely changed—the old is gone, the new has come (2 Cor. 5:17). Like changing clothes, we have "to take off [our] former way of life, the old self that is corrupted by deceitful desires, to be renewed in the spirit of [our] minds, and to put on the new self, the one created according to God's likeness in righteousness and purity of the truth" (Eph. 4:22-24).

Read 1 Corinthians 2:16 and note what Paul said about our minds.

God has given us a sound mind—He has given us the mind of Christ. We have the ability to understand God's Word,[31] see things from His viewpoint, and walk in His wisdom.[32] But to do so, we have to consistently fill our minds with His Word. Until we do, our minds will be full of everything life has thrown our way—especially the lies we believe about ourselves.

When Catherine was in kindergarten, she and a little boy in her class fought over a teddy bear. The boy got so angry with her that he ripped the bear from her hands and said, "Catherine Bobbie, you are dumb and ugly!"

What she did next astounds me to this day. The teacher told me Catherine squared her shoulders and said, "No, I'm not. My daddy says that I'm intelligent and beautiful!"

Nick has always affirmed our girls by reminding them daily of their worth and value. He is diligent to let them know the truth so they won't believe a lie.

Our heavenly Father wants us to know who He says we are so we won't fall for the lies we hear. When lies from the culture, our past, or hurtful things people have said cross our minds, let's learn how to respond like Catherine did. Let's start by saying, "My Daddy says ...," and then speak the Word to ourselves.

Read 2 Corinthians 10:3-5. What was Paul's instruction in verse 5b?

Paul made it clear that the battle for our minds is a spiritual one. The enemy, the devil, is the one Jesus called "a liar and the father of lies" (John 8:44). Since our battle is a spiritual one, we fight it with spiritual weapons—the truth of the gospel (Rom. 1:16) and the Word of God (Eph. 6:17). With those powerful weapons we can "demolish arguments and every proud thing that is raised up against the knowledge of God" and "take every thought captive to obey Christ" (2 Cor. 10:4b-5). Because of what God has done for us and who He says we are, we don't have to believe the lies.

Look up the following verses and remind yourself of what God says about you. Personalize each verse by beginning each statement with "I."

Psalm 34:5—I am ...

Psalm 139:13-14—I am ...

Isaiah 43:1-2—I am ...

John 1:12—I am ...

Ephesians 2:10—I am ...

Romans 6:6—I am ...

Romans 8:37—I am ...

1 Corinthians 6:19-20—I am ...

2 Corinthians 6:18—I am ...

Anything in opposition to what God's Word says about us is a lie. Is there something you've believed about yourself in the past that is contrary to God's Word?


How did learning the truth of God's Word refute those lies?


The lie I believed was that I wasn't enough. Ever. Of anything.

As God began to help me renew my mind with the truth by reading His Word, I realized more and more that what I thought about myself wasn't what He thought. So I began writing His thoughts (verses from the Bible) on sticky notes and putting them on my bedroom mirror, on the dash of my car, on my computer, inside the front cover of my Bible—anywhere I would see them as I went through my day. Even now I memorize verses to keep my mind thinking and believing the truth that sets me free, because it is only the truth we *know* that sets us free.

Look up John 8:31-32 and personalize it below.

We are not free to love others if we don't know the truth about ourselves. We are not free to see others as God sees them until we can see ourselves as God sees us. That's why we must look intently to His Word ...

- to be reminded that we are beautiful, valuable, and created as His beloved;
- to be reminded that Christ is in us, transforming us from the inside out.

We are God's daughters, and of all the titles we carry, we are more this one than any other. No other name given to us stands more permanent. No other title surpasses. Knowing we are a daughter turns our face unashamedly toward God. Knowing who we are changes the face we see in the mirror looking back at us. We are chosen, valuable, beautiful, secure, powerful—because we are in Christ.

When truth saturates our minds, our vision shifts, our hope emerges, and our love flows more freely.

# DAY 5

## *WHO IS MY NEIGHBOR?*

To love the Lord our God with all our hearts, souls, and minds isn't easy when our hearts have broken places, when our souls have wounds, and when our minds aren't renewed. But when we invite the Lord in to heal us and help us, He removes our blind spots so we can see—so we can love Him more fully and love others more freely. Isn't that the heart of seeing with 20/20 vision? To see those we may have been overlooking? Isn't this what Jesus wanted the religious leaders in Matthew 22:36 to grasp?

When the religious leaders asked Jesus, "Teacher, which command in the law is the greatest?" (Matt. 22:36), He said that loving God with all our hearts, souls, and minds is the ultimate commandment—and He could have stopped there, because He had answered the question. But He didn't. He went on to tell them the second greatest command: love your neighbor as yourself.

> Read Luke 10:25-37.

Whether you grew up in the church or not, most of you have probably heard some version of the good Samaritan story. Being too familiar with a passage of Scripture can hinder our ability to see truth. Unfamiliarity, though, helps us look harder and have our senses on high alert. In light of this, would you look at this story with me through a new set of lenses, as though it's unfamiliar to you? That way you won't miss what the Holy Spirit wants to show you.

This well-known parable is set in an isolated spot on a dangerous road in the Middle East known in Jesus' day as "The Ascent of Blood."[33] Violence was commonplace there. Like many before him, the traveling man was attacked by bandits, stripped, beaten, and left half dead.

To look more intently, let's review the facts of the story.

> Who were the first two people to see the man?

What action did they take?

Who was the third man to pass that way?

What was his response?

The religious people—the Jewish priest and the Levite who knew God's Word and had positions of authority in the synagogue—did nothing. They passed by on the other side.

The third man, who was neither a religious professional nor Jew, but was a native of Samaria, was moved with compassion and cared for the man.

All three were on their way somewhere else, but only one was willing to be interrupted and inconvenienced. Only one gave of his time and resources. And he happened to be a Samaritan—a man from a race and culture of people despised by the Jews.

Of the three men, only one loved as God loves, showing mercy and breaking down a barrier of prejudice and discrimination. The Samaritan loved his neighbor as himself.

According to verse 37b, what does Jesus want us to do?

If Jesus wants us to go and do the same, who in your sphere of influence would you describe as your neighbor? Think as broadly as possible. Think about your community. Who would you characterize as the oppressed? The marginalized? The discriminated? The poor? Who is it that others seem to reject? Or overlook? Make a list of everyone you identified.

I remember wondering how I would ever make a difference in the lives of victims of human trafficking. I had no resources, no contacts, no understanding, no strategy. I didn't know how human traffickers worked. I had no idea where to begin. I was simply compelled to do something, and I'm so thankful I didn't let anything stop me.

Have you been moved by compassion and stirred by God to do something but haven't yet? Why not?

If your reason is fear, what are you afraid of?

If it is a lack of knowledge or understanding, where could you turn to learn more?

If your reason is a lack of time to devote to the cause, are you simply too focused on yourself and your own family, career, or interests? Explain.

I know these are probing questions, but stopping to think and examine our hearts helps us to grow beyond where we are—and hopefully reignite what God is stirring in our hearts to do.

When I first became aware of human trafficking, God used the story of the good Samaritan to touch my heart and guide me into my future. I was preparing to speak from this text at a women's conference when God emphasized a phrase that I'd never paid much attention to before—"He went over to him" (Luke 10:34).

The more I studied, the more I couldn't stop reading that phrase. I found myself thinking about all the people in the world today who are like that man lying on the side of the road—heartbroken, wounded, and tormented. I thought of people left behind by abuse, addiction, imprisonment, loss, famine, disease, violence, tyranny, and oppression. I thought of people broken by injustice, ravaged by war, stripped of their belongings, dignity, identity, and self-worth. And I thought about all the missing women and children I had seen on posters in a regional airport in Thessaloniki, Greece. They were the ones God wanted to really draw my attention to.[34]

I couldn't help but notice in the text that Jesus never said the priest and the Levite were bad people. So, to me it seemed they were simply busy, religious people. People so consumed with keeping their schedules, appointments, and commitments they ended up walking past someone they should have helped.

I was deeply moved when I realized they probably considered the man lying on the side of the road to be an interruption to their ministry, not the reason for it.

Suddenly, I felt more like the religious people in the text than the Samaritan. I was so busy running from conference to conference that I was in danger of seeing the missing women and children, the victims of human trafficking, as an interruption to my ministry rather than the purpose for it.

See what I mean about allowing God to bring a familiar passage to life? I had read the story of the good Samaritan dozens of times, but that day in my hotel room as I prepared to speak later that night, I looked and saw what the text was saying to me personally. And everything changed.

I was a busy woman—a wife and a mother of two with plenty to do. I didn't need another venture; and yet, it was clear God wanted to interrupt my plans for His purpose. God wanted me to cross the road for people I'd never met, never knew existed, and never knew were missing. He wanted me to go find the missing men, women, and children trapped in modern-day slavery.

Isn't that what the good Samaritan did? He crossed the road. He went out of his way. His compassion moved him to action.

Is there someone God is asking you to cross the road for right now? Someone, perhaps, you would normally steer away from? Would you define that person as your neighbor?

We are never to withhold our compassion. Throughout Scripture God describes people who are in need and what our response to them should be. Look up the following verses and note who your neighbor is in each passage.

**Proverbs 14:31**

**Proverbs 19:17**

**Proverbs 21:13**

**James 1:27**

The victims of human trafficking are my neighbors, as are the people I meet in churches, the families who live next door, and the homeless people on the street. The person who needs something I can provide is my neighbor.

If we are to reach our world, then we need to see that everyone is our neighbor. Every person is worthy of love regardless of their beliefs, actions, or attitudes, because God sees them as lovable and redeemable by His grace. They are all people made in His image. But we won't go to them if we let fear stop us before we ever start, if we let the "what-ifs" consume us, or our well-meaning, spiritual activities take precedence. Those things blind us and choke out God's promptings.

We've dug deep this week, inviting God in to heal our broken hearts, wounded souls, and distracted minds. I think that would spark courage in us to go one more step and identify what might be holding us back from loving our neighbor as ourselves.

What's God showing you? What's stopping you from starting?

It's time to cross the road.

## ZOOM IN

The more we know and feel we are loved by God, the more love we show.

The more we know and feel the mercy of God, the more merciful we are.

The more we know and feel the forgiveness of God, the more forgiving we are.

The more we know and feel the grace of God, the more grace we give.

The more we know and feel the goodness of God, the more goodness we extend.

The more we know and feel the kindness of God, the kinder we are.

The more we know and feel the peace of God, the more peace we emanate.

Thank you for hanging in and being willing to "go there," wherever "there" is in your heart, soul, and mind this week. Thank you for being willing to allow God to interrupt your life for His plans and purposes. I'm proud of you for being so willing to see who your neighbor is, to go to them, and to love them as you love yourself.

As we get ready to step into next week, remember to keep praying for the harvest and for that person you want to be found. Our fervent prayers avail much (Jas. 5:16)!

## WEEK 4

# SPREAD YOUR
# FRAGRANCE

# REFRAME YOUR VIEW

## WATCH

Watch Video Week 4, *Citizens of Heaven, Residents of Earth*, and record your personal thoughts as you watch and listen.

## DISCUSS

I have an Australian passport because I was born there. I have an American passport because I became a citizen of America. I now have dual citizenship. But, spiritually, I can have only one citizenship. Because I have been born again, I am a citizen of the kingdom of heaven. I now have new rights and privileges—the ones afforded a daughter of the King. But how can I live on this earth and be a citizen of heaven at the same time? This is a spiritual perspective that God wants us to understand. It is a concept the early Christians in Philippi understood, and it's something we can learn from them today.

Pause for a moment. Look over your notes. What stood out to you from the video teaching?

Based on the video teaching, describe the similarities between the Christians who lived in Philippi in the first century and Christians living in the world today.

What did Paul mean when he said our citizenship is in heaven? How do you become a citizen of heaven?

What does it mean to speak as ambassadors on behalf of King Jesus? Would you say you're representing the King well? Why or why not?

Would you say your current perspective on life is more temporal or eternal? Explain.

Does your earthly conduct—your actions, words, decisions—reflect your heavenly citizenship? If so, how? If not, why not?

Let's bring a glimpse of heaven to earth. Let's live our lives as citizens of heaven and ambassadors on earth—as representatives of God's kingdom right where we are.

## MOVE

List ideas for how you can accomplish the assignment God has given you as an ambassador.

Choose one or two of those ideas to put into practice this week.

## PRAY

Heavenly Father, I want my heart to be so invested in heaven that I care more than I ever have about what happens here, where You have sent me. Show me how to bring more kindness, love, compassion, and goodness to this earth. Show me how to reach people who have never known what it is to be a citizen of heaven. Help me to bring a glimpse of heaven to earth everywhere You send me.

# DAY 1

## *WHAT'S YOUR SIGNATURE SCENT?*

I have an obsession with smells.

Some of my favorites are fresh flowers, moussaka right out of the oven, and olive trees. What can I say? Even my olfactory nerve knows I'm Greek!

Whether a vanilla candle or a waft of fresh ground coffee, a beautiful aroma can make me instantly happy. On the other hand, if I walk into a room in our home and the smell is dull—or repugnant with volleyball practice shorts and dirty sneakers—I feel compelled to grab a can of air freshener and go running through the house.

I find it fascinating how scents can affect us. When we want to feel better we can light a candle, and it changes the entire atmosphere around us. There is no doubt that smells can evoke strong emotions and influence us significantly. And the marketing industry knows it! That's why there is such a thing as scent branding. Companies invest hundreds of millions of dollars in infusing their environments with specific scents to draw people to their products.[35]

Smells are powerful. They have the power to jog our memories, quickly taking us back to a season of time or a familiar place in our lives. They can even bring flashbacks that throw us into the arms of loved ones gone long ago.

To this day, if I pass a perfume counter, I cannot resist aromatizing myself in Chanel N°5. My mother wore it all of my life. She always smelled divine to me. In my memories, my mum was Chanel N°5, and Chanel N°5 was my mum. There's just no separating the two. Just by spritzing myself I can smell her walking in the front door with a load of groceries in her arms, and if I let the memory of her smell linger a bit longer, then I can begin to see the sparkle in her eyes and hear the joy in her laugh.

My dad, on the other hand, was a different story. Dad was far more basic. He was an Old Spice man, steady and dependable.

Just like my mum was Chanel N°5, most girls have a signature scent. Do you? If so, what's yours?

Now I know what you're thinking: *What do smell and scent have to do with God, our faith, and reaching the lost?* More than you might imagine!

Do you know there are numerous references to smells and smelling in God's Word? For example, the phrase "pleasing aroma to the Lord" appears more than forty times in the Old Testament.[36]

Smells matter to God. Look up the following verses and note the occasion and instruction.

Genesis 8:21

Exodus 30:34-38

Numbers 15:3

Even in the New Testament God shows us the power of fragrant aromas. Read Philippians 4:18 and write how Paul described the sacrificial offering of the Philippians.

What astounded me the most in my research—and what I can't wait for you to discover—is that God is into scent branding. While companies scent-brand their spaces and environments, He scent-brands His people. No, it's not quite like the Chanel N°5 my mum wore, or the Old Spice my dad wore. It's not like my favorite fragrance or yours. It's even better.

Read 2 Corinthians 2:14-16 below and underline the words *aroma* and *fragrance* every time you see them.

> [14] But thanks be to God, who always leads us in Christ's triumphal procession and through us spreads the aroma of the knowledge of him in every place.

> [15] For to God we are the fragrance of Christ among those who are being saved and among those who are perishing.

> [16] To some we are an aroma of death leading to death, but to others, an aroma of life leading to life. Who is adequate for these things?

God has given us His signature scent—the aroma of Christ. But why? To better understand God's purpose in this, let's walk through the verses.

When Paul cited Christ's triumphal procession (v. 14), the Corinthians would have associated the reference to the Roman triumphs of the day. These were spectacular celebration parades held in Rome for military commanders who had won an important victory on the battlefield.[37] On the morning of these parades, the Roman priests would burn volumes of incense in bonfires lit on the seven hills surrounding Rome. When Roman citizens awoke to the smell of incense, they awoke to the smell of victory.[38]

Paul used this as an example of the Christian life, because Jesus is our victorious General. He came to this earth and conquered the enemy, sin, and death at the cross. He is our resurrected Savior. He is triumphant, and the sweet smell of victory forever lingers on Him—and us!

When the Roman citizens awoke to the smell of incense, and then smelled it at the parade, surely it caused the day and its victory to be etched into their memories. Smells can do that to us, can't they?

When the parade came to an end and everyone walked back home, the Corinthians probably took the lingering scent of the incense with them. I imagine as they entered their houses and walked from room to room, they dispersed the fragrance, leaving a sweet aroma throughout the house.

How might the aroma of the knowledge of Christ linger in the places we visit or in the minds of the people we meet?

Read verse 15 again. It seems we emit a particular kind of smell to God. Have you ever thought about the fact that God can smell? How does this verse describe our smell to God?

We are the fragrance of Christ here on this earth among those who are being saved and those who are perishing. But we smell differently to each group.

Read verse 16 again. What do we smell like to those who are perishing?

What do we smell like to those who are saved?

The incense of the Roman parade smelled wonderful to the Roman army and to the people of Rome. It was the smell of victory. But to the prisoners of war the smell represented defeat, slavery, and death. In like fashion, Christians are a sweet aroma to those who know Christ or are coming to Christ as we share the gospel. But to those who reject Christ, we are a very different aroma.

Though we are a sweet fragrance to those who are being saved, I have to wonder if at times our aroma grows a bit stale and we don't even realize it. It happens too easily to all of us. We get busy. We get offended or wounded. And suddenly our fragrance that once suggested a bright floral or perky citrus smells more like dirty sneakers.

What if we've started spending too much time with people who are stinky? To the point that their stink overpowers our aroma? Yes, we absolutely want to be in the world, rubbing elbows with the people God brings across our path, but we also want to ensure that the aroma of Christ in us overpowers the aroma of the world around us.

Look up the following verses and record what ensures that we will stay fragrant.

**Ephesians 5:1-2**

**Colossians 3:12**

**Philippians 2:3**

These instructions and many more like them help us know how to continue to impact our world with the aroma of Christ—to fulfill the Great Commission to go and make disciples. It's His fragrance in us—that first whiff—that people are drawn to.

That's what we'll talk about tomorrow. But for now, enjoy knowing God has given you His signature scent—the aroma of Christ—and it's His will that you smell divine!

# DAY 2

## *TIME FOR A SCRATCH AND SNIFF TEST*

Flying as much as I do, I've learned to tolerate all kinds of smells—the tuna sandwich someone brings on board, the baby's diaper that needs changing, and the fellow who drank coffee before boarding. For him, I have great grace. I only wish he'd brought me a cup.

But there's one smell I've never adjusted to: the smell of people's feet when they slip off their shoes and stretch out for a nap on a fourteen-hour flight to Sydney from Los Angeles. I realize they have no idea the effect they are having on me and everyone around them. I'm sure they are not harboring a grudge against their fellow … although, they are provoking one. Despite my desire to be understanding, I always find that I have no words—though I feel sure, given the opportunity without the threat of being restrained by an air marshal, I could think of some.

Watch yourself, now. Don't judge. You know that if you found yourself in the same set of circumstances, you might want to enlighten a fellow passenger as well. We all know that self-awareness is powerful, and when we're lacking it, we need a sister to help us out! Amirite?

In all seriousness, sometimes I think we all need to take a scratch and sniff test every now and then.

Remember those cute little scratch and sniff books? We had several when my girls were small. I remember how they couldn't wait for me to finish reading each page so they could scratch and sniff the smelly spot. Even after the books were totally worn out and all I could smell was an occasional whiff of cardboard, they still scratched and sniffed as though we had just bought the book.

In the same way, I think we need to rub shoulders with a trusted friend and ask them how we smell. What if we don't smell as sweet as we think we do? What if our scent has worn off? What if the way we actually smell to our families, our coworkers, even complete strangers is completely different than what we think?

When we walk into a room, do people smell …

- ☐ integrity or hypocrisy?
- ☐ life or death?
- ☐ graciousness or unforgiveness?
- ☐ confidence or anxiety?
- ☐ selflessness or selfishness?
- ☐ hope or despair?

- ☐ humility or pride?
- ☐ peace or chaos?
- ☐ joy or depression?
- ☐ acceptance or rejection?
- ☐ love or anger?
- ☐ encouragement or condemnation?

You mean people can smell *all* that? In a sense, yes! Have you ever heard someone say, "You could smell fear all over them"? It's a figure of speech, but it conveys a very real meaning. We can sense—we can smell—when something has gone from a sweet fragrance to a sour scent.

Can't people smell us …

- when our disappointments and failures have grown into bitterness;
- when our hurts have turned into festering wounds;
- when our insecurity has turned into jealousy;
- when our faith has turned into fear?

God has placed in each of us His signature scent—the aroma of Christ—but do you think it's possible to mask His scent? How?

When was a time you smelled or sensed the emotions of someone?

When was a time you became aware that you reeked of some strong emotion or attitude? How did that affect those around you?

During a recent summer vacation, Sophia and I spent an afternoon learning how to make perfume. For four hours we were tutored by a chemical engineer who explained the mystery of how scents are a perfect blend of art and science—and how even one slight change in chemicals can completely alter a formula and the subsequent bouquet.

I learned that many perfumes are made by pressing and crushing flowers, fruits, grasses, spices, wood, and a myriad of other strong-smelling substances. The purpose of the pressing or crushing is to extract the natural oils. In ancient times, the oils were extracted, pressed, steamed, and then burned to scent the surrounding air. Today, the oils are extracted with much more modern methods, mixed with chemicals to enhance the smell, and then left to mature for a period of time before they are ready to be marketed. The creation of a scent is a lengthy process that involves multiple stages: compressing, crushing, steaming, boiling, mixing, and even curating for days, weeks, or months.

After the class, I couldn't help but think how the sweet fragrance of Christ comes forth as we endure the pressures of life and mature in our faith when we are tested, tried, and refined.

> Look up the following verses and write how you've been through similar processes in your own life.
>
> **Romans 5:3-5**
>
> **2 Corinthians 4:8-12**
>
> **Hebrews 12:4-12**
>
> **James 1:2-4**

It's easier to endure the painful process of healing when I understand that on the other side is a beautiful fragrance—one that positively influences the world.

> Think about the last time you invited Jesus to heal a festering wound. How did Jesus bring about healing? How did He change your scent?

Our untreated and unhealed wounds can conceal the sweet-smelling fragrance of Christ. But when we allow Jesus to heal us, we are able to express more compassion, more empathy, more patience, and more love to others.

Over the course of the thirty years I've walked with Jesus, the more healing I've embraced, the more fragrant the aroma I have exuded in my marriage, mothering, and ministry life. It's Christ in me that brings encouragement and hope to others.

When was a time you prayed for and persevered with someone until his or her stench of pain was replaced with the sweet smell of Jesus?

I'll ask again, because I want you to truly be aware: How do you smell? Jot down some thoughts about the kind of fragrance you're exuding at home, at school, at work, and other situations in which you find yourself.

Smells don't lie. If we've worked out, eaten garlic, or gone fishing, there is a smell we carry. What about when we spend time with Jesus?

Read Acts 4:13. What did the Jewish leaders sense about the apostles?

Standing on trial before the religious leaders, Peter and John exuded boldness, faith, confidence, and wisdom. It was evident they had been with Jesus.

Is it evident you've been with Jesus? Why or why not?

Is your signature scent a little sweeter since starting this Bible study? How did you smell before starting? Explain.

There's a story in the Bible that shows how a stench can be replaced by a fragrant aroma. John 11:1-38 records the story of Lazarus's death. Four days after his death and burial, Jesus arrived on the scene, and when He did, Lazarus's sister, Martha, told Jesus in verse 39, "Lord, there is already a stench because he has been dead four days." Nonetheless, Jesus called to him to come out of the tomb; He raised Lazarus from the dead (John 11:43-44).

Read John 12:1-3. Describe what Mary did a few days later.

It's interesting that this family had gone from the stench of death to the beautiful fragrance of love for Christ.

The entire atmosphere in their home was filled with the fragrant scent of Mary's act of worship. Because she spent time at the feet of Jesus, pouring out all her perfume, it changed the smell in the room. I would think even when she stood and walked away, she carried the scent of her devotion to Jesus on her hair and skin. She took the smell of sweet perfume with her.

When I was growing up, I could walk through our house and know which rooms Mum had passed through, all because of her scent. In the same way, the aroma of our lives should be evidence that we've spent time with Jesus. Our signature fragrance should make our Christian faith unmistakable.

Is your faith memorable to others? How so?

I understand we can't say much about our faith in our schools and workplaces sometimes, but nothing can stop us from diffusing the sweet fragrance of the gospel to everyone we meet. As we close out today, ask God to help you leave a sweet aroma wherever you go.

# DAY 3

## *BE THEN DO*

As much as I loved my mother's signature scent, what I truly loved and will always miss is her natural scent—the smell that was genetically hers and hers alone. The one God created her to wear that no soap could ever wash off. Maybe you remember your mother's or your grandmother's. Natural scents of women who loved us are hard to forget and easy to cherish.

We all have a scent like that—and no two people have the same one.[39] It's something we're destined to have and can never escape. It's part of who we are, regardless of what we do or where we go.

But our spiritual scent is something that can change, become stronger, and become more effective. The more time we spend with God, the more we will reflect the character and nature of God. The more we allow God to transform us from the inside out, the more we will emit the aroma of Christ.

Emitting the fragrance of Christ is like so much of our Christian journey—it's about *being* instead of *doing*. We are to be the aroma of Christ, and out of that being, then do. But sometimes we get this out of order. In our busy lives we naturally focus more on doing instead of being. When that happens, our Christian lives become one more thing to check off our list instead of something fresh, growing, and effective that is an outflow of our time with Jesus.

> What areas in your Christian life have you inadvertently swapped *being* for *doing*?

Is it possible that's what we've done with the concept of witnessing to others about our faith? Have we taken something God has called us to be and turned it into something we have to do? And because it is so uncomfortable, we find ourselves avoiding it altogether?

Too often, I think we experience fear of sharing our faith primarily because we've misunderstood the many ways God wants us to share it. God has called us to be witnesses, to spread "the aroma of the knowledge of [Christ] in every place" (2 Cor. 2:14).

Wait, did I just feel you tense up? Does the word *witness* evoke anxiety in you? Give me five more minutes, and I promise to alleviate your stress! Let me explain what God says about being a witness. I think you may find His perspective surprising.

Look up Acts 1:8. Because this is such a pivotal verse, I want you to write it out completely. Then circle or highlight where Jesus calls us witnesses.

*Jesus has called us to be witnesses, not to do witnessing.*

Go back and look at exactly what Jesus said in this verse: He has called us to *be* witnesses, not to *do* witnessing.

And yet, in being a witness there will come a time when we will want to do, because it's a natural outflow of our being. At some point, because we smell so good, someone will ask why, and we'll want to tell them.

Let's unpack what it means to be a witness.

What comes to mind when you think of the word *witness*? Do you imagine the role of a witness in a court of law? Or a religious endeavor? Or something altogether different?

## wit·ness

1. person who sees an event, typically a crime or accident, take place.[40]

In a judicial system, a witness is someone who has relevant information about an event. As they take the stand, they take an oath to "tell the truth, the whole truth and nothing but the truth, so help me, God," and then they share what they know.

Look up Proverbs 14:25 and record why a witness should tell the truth.

Did you catch that? A truthful witness saves lives. Isn't that what God wants us to do? Isn't that what we want to do?

In a court of law, a truthful witness recounts what happened to help the judge or jury clarify events. This person bears witness to the truth.

Let's look up a few verses about how we bear witness to the truth. As you read each verse, notice who is bearing witness and to what or to whom.

Acts 10:43

Acts 15:7-9

Romans 8:15-17

Even Jesus bore witness to the truth. Look up John 18:37 and write what Jesus said to Pilate.

From all you just read, is bearing witness more about being or doing, or both? Explain.

Bearing witness to the truth requires an alignment between our beliefs and our actions—always. In light of this, can you think of how people know what we believe even when we don't speak?

Look up 1 Peter 2:12. We'll look at this verse in more depth later in the week, but for now, note what Peter said about our beliefs and actions being in alignment. Note what he said about us being witnesses.

## ZOOM IN

When Nick and I started following Christ, long before we met, our families didn't know how to process our decisions. We were both raised in churches with centuries-old traditions, and now, we were serving in a contemporary church. To say it was a culture shock to our families doesn't begin to describe it. And when we married, their disapproval didn't stop. We've both sat at many holiday dinners feeling the concern of our relatives who thought we were going to witness to them by preaching to them. But we never did. We just loved them for who they were, right where they were. We did our best to be a sweet-smelling aroma, a witness of the love and goodness of God.

Twenty-five years later—after twenty-five years of holiday dinners— most of our relatives have reached out to us for prayer, for answers to their questions, and for a more meaningful relationship with God. They've invited us in to share with them about our faith and why it's so important to us. All because we were witnesses rather than people who did witnessing. All because we chose to love first and talk second.

When we bear witness to the truth we stand up for truth, we represent truth, and our lives reflect that we live by truth—whether we speak or not. Yet, living it and speaking it are both actions.

Which do you find easier—talking the talk or walking the walk? Why?

List ways you can bear witness to the truth with your family, your children, your friends, and your colleagues. Include ideas that involve speaking and living. Do they both require action? Explain.

In our court systems, there are different kinds of witnesses who testify to the truth.

Character witnesses testify to the accused person's character. They might give testimony of how long they have known the accused in order to establish the individual's good reputation, or they might give examples of when he or she demonstrated moral conduct.

Expert witnesses are specialists educated in a certain field. They testify with respect to their area of expertise. They interpret the facts and then give their opinions based on those facts.

Lay witnesses—the most common type—have personally observed something relevant to the case and can give a firsthand description of the events. This could be a bystander, or a passerby at the scene, or the arresting officer.[41]

From a spiritual perspective, which type of witness do you think Jesus wants us to be and why?

In some ways, we're to be all three kinds. Do you agree or disagree?

Being a witness is a life God has called us to live. At times we'll have the opportunity to give voice to that calling, and at times we'll simply live a life that exudes the aroma of Christ.

Read 1 Corinthians 3:7-9. How does this passage apply to the different ways we can be witnesses?

Are there times we might have more influence by holding off speaking to someone about our faith initially? Give some examples.

Take a moment and list the people you want to see come to Christ. Then jot down how long you've been a sweet-smelling aroma of Christ in their lives.

Over time, have you seen them soften, be more receptive, or reach toward Jesus? Explain.

I'm never happier than when I get to testify of Jesus. And yet, I understand the power of being a witness who walks the walk when I am not talking—especially in a generation that is more lost than found. We must understand that at all times, we are witnesses. That's why God wants us to be before we do.

As for giving voice to being a witness, God has a plan for how we can do it and do it well! That's what we'll dive into tomorrow.

# DAY 4
## *THE HOLY SPIRIT HELPS US*

I often find myself in situations where someone needs encouragement. I want to be faith-filled, helpful, and kind, but honestly, I have no idea what to say. Surely you've been in a similar situation. When this happens, I do the only thing I know to do—I pray fervently for God to quickly drop a thought into my mind. It's painful knowing someone is desperate to hear something encouraging but you're struggling to find the words.

Not long ago, I had one of those moments—and, as always, God was faithful to help me. I was at the nail salon where I had been intentionally going for about a year—all in an effort to develop a friendship with Vivian, the manicurist I met on my first visit. Over several months, as she polished my nails, we talked about everything—what's for dinner, the latest buzz in local news, and of course, which polish color I should pick. We exchanged stories of our families and holiday celebrations and shared our experiences of raising daughters. I always looked forward to chatting it up with her and laughing about anything and everything.

On this particular visit, I noticed she didn't seem her normal cheerful self. When I casually asked her how her week was going, she unexpectedly opened up to me in a way she hadn't before. She began telling me more about her daughter—slowly at first, and then, to my shock, she unloaded the most tragic news.

Vivian's daughter was a second-year law student, and, after battling depression, she committed suicide—apparently since my last appointment. I had sat with this woman so many times and talked about so many everyday events, and suddenly she was bringing me into unfathomable pain and grief too heavy for any mother to carry. I couldn't begin to comprehend how she was even able to work. She had shown me pictures of her daughter a few months back, and it was evident how proud she was. At first, all I could do was hold her and weep with her. I couldn't imagine the depth of her pain, but the compassion of God flooded my heart as I wrapped my arms around her. As she choked out more of the story, I just listened and loved her. I couldn't let go of her. And I couldn't miss how helpless she felt ... and how helpless I felt.

I wanted to do more, but what? I needed help to know what to do and say in that moment.

Sometimes, the most daunting part of being a witness is feeling totally blind-sided by a situation, not knowing what to say or how to say it. As I sat with Vivian, I desperately needed wisdom, grace, and truth.

God gave me words that day, and as I continued to visit her over the following months, He gave me more. Vivian was very open to talking about eternity, and God was faithful to guide me in what to say and when to say it.

When have you been at a loss for words in a similar situation?

How did you navigate that situation? Did you ask for God's help? If so, how did He lead you?

God helps us in those situations through the power of the Holy Spirit.

Read John 16:7 and write it in the space provided below.

Jesus was trying to help prepare His disciples for His imminent departure from the earth. Notice He didn't say someone better was coming, just that it would be better for Him to go, because He was leaving them the Holy Spirit, someone who would be in every one of them at all times—to help them in every situation.

Nonetheless, can you imagine how devastating this news must have felt to His disciples? From their perspective, what could possibly be better than God incarnate walking the earth with them?

But they would soon understand that Jesus wasn't abandoning them; rather, God was sending the Holy Spirit to help them—and us.

Read Acts 1:4-5. How did Jesus describe the Holy Spirit?

Write down what the following verses say about the Holy Spirit.

**2 Corinthians 1:21-22**

**2 Corinthians 5:5**

**Ephesians 1:13-14**

**Ephesians 4:30**

The Holy Spirit is a gift of God. He is the Father's promise. The Holy Spirit takes up residence in those of us who are in Christ. He has been given to us as a seal—a guarantee—of our future in Christ and with Christ. What great news!

**ZOOM IN**
The Greek word for Holy Spirit is *parakletos*. It appears four times in John's Gospel (14:16; 14:26; 15:26; 16:7) and once in 1 John 2:1. It literally means "one who pleads another's cause before a judge, a pleader, counsel for defense, legal assistant, an advocate, a comforter."[42]

Look up the following verses and record the different ways Jesus said the Holy Spirit is to have influence in our lives.

**John 14:16**

**John 14:26**

**John 16:7-8**

**John 16:13**

**Acts 1:8**

The Holy Spirit guides us. He teaches us. He reminds us. He empowers us to fulfill God's purposes and plans. He is the One God sent to come alongside us and help us to be all God has called us to be—ambassadors, citizens of heaven, and witnesses to the truth.

The Holy Spirit is our helper. He wants to help us. But for help to be actualized, it must not only be extended, it must also be accepted.

How can we accept the Holy Spirit's help?

Throughout the Book of Acts, the Holy Spirit led Christ followers to fulfill the Great Commission. One of these Christ followers was Philip—commonly called Philip the Evangelist to distinguish him from Philip the apostle.

Read Acts 8:26-39. What did the Holy Spirit tell Philip to do?

*People associate being loved with being listened to.*

The Holy Spirit told Philip to "go and join that chariot" (v. 29), and Philip went. One way the Holy Spirit helps us is by prompting us. He may prompt us to go to that place. To say hello to that person. To walk across the street and introduce ourselves to that neighbor. To take the initiative to get to know that student or that coworker. We accept the Spirit's help when we say yes to His promptings.

When Philip caught up to the man, he started a conversation. Look at verse 30 and write what Philip said.

I find this verse so fascinating! Philip's first words to the man were a question. Philip took the time to ask and to listen, to understand what was going on in his life. What was true then is true today. Several studies have found that people associate being loved with being listened to. Imagine the fragrance of Christ we would emit by taking a genuine interest in others—by simply asking questions and listening to what they share.

As Philip listened, the Holy Spirit opened a door. The man raised a question about what he was reading, and, starting with that verse, Philip told him the good news about Jesus.

I'm so glad Jesus didn't leave us to be witnesses on our own. I depended on the Holy Spirit that day as I held Vivian while we both wept. As I leaned into the Spirit, He gave me words of compassion, empathy, love, hope, and mercy. Because I had lived out my life before her as a witness in the previous year—because my words aligned with my actions—she welcomed me being there for her in that moment. And she was open to hearing what I had to say from that day forward.

Knowing how much the Holy Spirit helps me, I can see why Jesus didn't send anyone to fulfill the Great Commission until He sent the Holy Spirit. We cannot be witnesses in our own power and wisdom.

Philip is mentioned again in Acts 21:8-9, which takes place several years later. Read these verses and record how Philip is described.

Philip's reputation as a leader in the early church and as a proclaimer of the gospel remained intact. Don't we all want to be found faithful witnesses years from now?

Look up the following verses and note how the Holy Spirit helped the first believers carry out God's purposes.

Acts 6:1-10

Acts 10:17-22

Acts 13:1-3

If the early believers who walked with Jesus needed the Holy Spirit to be effective witnesses, then how much more do we need the Holy Spirit to do what we could never do on our own? Take a moment right now to pray and ask for the empowerment of the Holy Spirit to help you be the witness God has called you to be in your world.

# DAY 5

## *THE SMELL OF FRESH FRUIT*

This week, we've discussed fragrances and scents and smells. We've discussed how, through us, God is spreading "the aroma of the knowledge of him in every place" (2 Cor. 2:14). And how the more time we spend with Jesus, the better we reflect Him and the more enhanced this aroma becomes. I want to take our discussion a step further and talk about another scent we carry—the scent of His fruit in our lives.

While preparing to write this study, I had the opportunity to teach in Naples, Italy. (Some invitations you need to pray about, but at other times, you know right away it is the will of God in Christ Jesus that you go—and this was definitely one of those times!) During our visit, our hosts took us on a tour of Naples and the surrounding region. As we drove past a rocky hillside, I instantly smelled the lemon trees laden with fruit, and then I caught sight of them.

Immediately I was able to tell they were lemon trees. Not because of their branches or leaves, but because of their fruit. That's the easiest way to tell one tree from another.

Isn't that just how God's fruit is in our lives? Isn't it evidence of whose we are and who we are?

> Jesus said we would be able to distinguish people by their fruit. Look up Matthew 7:15-20 and write down what you think He meant by the word *fruit*.

> Jesus said we are to bear fruit—good fruit—but how? Look up John 15:1-5 and write down the key to bearing good fruit.

The key is to remain in Jesus. Some translations say "abide" in Him. If a branch abides in the vine, then it's receiving all the nourishment the vine provides.

What are some ways we can ensure that we're abiding in Christ?

When we spend time with Jesus—in His Word, in worship, in prayer, and in a local church community—we remain in Him. We trust Him, learn from Him, grow in Him, and the result is that we become more like Him.

What is the fruit we produce by abiding in Him? It's not outward success or external results we can claim as our own but spiritual qualities, behaviors, and works brought about by God's power in us and through us—true righteousness (Phil. 1:11), praise (Heb. 13:15), sacrificial love in meeting needs (Rom. 15:28), leading people to Christ (Rom. 1:13), and what we're going to focus on today: Christian character.

There is a specific list in Galatians 5:22-23 of the fruit God wants to produce in us. Look up these verses and list the fruit below.

1.
2.
3.
4.
5.
6.
7.
8.
9.

Much has been written about the fruit of the Spirit, including an extensive study by my friend and fellow LifeWay author, Beth Moore.[43] What I want us to high-light in our study today is how our flourishing in the fruit of the Spirit can further spread the aroma of Christ. To begin, let's dig deeper into the meaning of each fruit, paying the most attention to how the fruit we produce can impact the lost we bump into every day.

## LOVE

The Greek word for love in Galatians 5:22 is *agape*.[44] It's the highest form of love used in the New Testament. It denotes a love that is unconditional—no strings attached. It's the love spoken of in John 3:16.

We live in a world that isn't used to a love that gives without expecting anything in return. But that's exactly the kind of love God has called us to give.

Read 1 John 3:18. How are we to love?

While the context of this command is how believers are to love one another, it certainly applies to the whole world. Our love is to be demonstrated in action.

Think of the people in your world who are lost and need to be found. What is one way you can love them with action and truth, one way you can give to them without expecting anything in return?

*Agape* love expressed through us can soften people's hearts to hear the gospel.

## JOY

Joy is equivalent to gladness in our hearts. It's not based on our circumstances or external conditions.

How does your joy help your witness to a lost and dying world?

Joy is most evident in our lives when we praise God all the way through a hard situation, not just at the end when it's resolved. When we praise Him at all times, we stand out in a world that bases its joy on circumstances.

## PEACE

Peace comes from the Greek word *eirene*. The Hebrew equivalent is *shalom*.[45] *Eirene* expresses a tranquility in our soul that isn't affected by outward pressures or circumstances. It's an inner stability not easily upset.

According to John 14:27, Jesus gives us this kind of peace. With the peace of Jesus, we can watch the nightly news and all its reports of active shooters, war, riots, and threats of chaos, and still have complete peace even though there are plenty of reasons to feel afraid.

> How can you share the peace of Christ with your loved ones, friends, coworkers, and neighbors as they walk through difficult times?

## PATIENCE

The Greek word for patience is *makrothymia*.[46] In some Bibles it's translated as "longsuffering." *Makrothymia* relates to a candle that has a very long wick and is prepared to burn for a long time.

> When was the last time you had the opportunity to develop the fruit of patience? On the freeway? In the checkout line? Write about the last time you felt stretched to your limit.

> How can your being patient with the people around you affect their interest in Jesus?

## KINDNESS

Kindness comes from the Greek word *chrestos*, meaning "serviceable" or "to be friendly toward others."[47] When applied to our relationships, kindness implies being adaptable to others. When we become adaptable to the needs of those around us rather than requiring them to adapt to us, it softens them.

Read 1 Corinthians 9:20-22 and note all the ways Paul adapted himself to others.

Did you notice how Paul was in the world but not of it? He was among the people in the world, reaching them where they were.

What opportunities do you have to display kindness in being adaptable? How can you be "all things to all people" so that you might "by every possible means save some" (1 Cor. 9:22)?

## GOODNESS

Goodness in the Greek is *agathosyne*. This word portrays a person who is generous, big-hearted, and charitable.[48]

Read Acts 10:38 and describe how Jesus walked in goodness.

How can you do good at work, at school, and in your community? Make a list and choose two or three things to do this week.

## FAITHFULNESS

"Jesus Christ is the same yesterday, today, and forever" (Heb. 13:8). He doesn't change (Mal. 3:6; Jas. 1:17). He is faithful (Heb. 10:23).

In the Galatians 5 passage, the Greek word for faithfulness is *pistis*. It means the quality of being true, trustworthy, and reliable in your dealings with people.[49]

What does it look like practically to be a faithful person? How can faithfulness make a difference in our relationships with unbelievers?

## GENTLENESS

A person who exhibits gentleness demonstrates kindness and goodness of heart.[50] This person is forbearing, patient, slow to respond in anger, and in control of himself in the face of insults or injuries.

The same Greek root for gentleness is used in Matthew 11:29, where Jesus described Himself as "lowly."

Read Matthew 11:29. How have you experienced the gentleness of Jesus?

How important is gentleness as you love and relate to the lost?

## SELF-CONTROL

A close cousin of gentleness is self-control, which is having power over one's self. It can also be defined as having control or restraint of one's passions, appetites, and desires.[51] Someone with self-control maintains a life of discipline and moderation.

Where do you see evidence of self-control in your life? Where do you see a need for greater self-control?

If you were to walk in more self-control, how do you think it would affect those you're hoping to see come to Christ?

God has called us to abide in Him and be the fragrant fruit of the Spirit to our world. Second Peter 1:5-7 tells us to add attributes to our faith, which implies we need to be constantly developing and growing:

For this very reason, make every effort to supplement your faith with goodness, goodness with knowledge, knowledge with self-control, self-control with endurance, endurance with godliness, godliness with brotherly affection, and brotherly affection with love.

Read 2 Peter 1:8 and fill in the blanks below:

"For if you possess these qualities in _____ _____, they will keep you from being _____ and _____ in your knowledge of our Lord Jesus Christ."

Imagine the difference we could make in people's lives if everywhere we went, we spread …

- love in the midst of indifference;
- joy in the midst of sorrow;
- peace in the midst of chaos;
- patience in the midst of frenzy;
- kindness in the midst of cruelty;
- goodness in the midst of selfishness;
- faithfulness in the midst of carelessness;
- gentleness in the midst of hardness;
- self-control in the midst of a world spiraling out of control.[52]

I know today was a lot of study, and I'm proud of you for all your hard work this week. Well done! Now it's time to go out into your world and spread your fragrance.

**WEEK 5**

# TALK ABOUT JESUS

## REFRAME YOUR VIEW

### WATCH

Watch Video Week 5, *Magnify His Story in Your Story,* and record your personal thoughts as you listen.

_____

_____

_____

_____

_____

_____

_____

_____

_____

_____

_____

_____

_____

_____

_____

_____

_____

_____

## DISCUSS

When Jesus was on His way to Galilee from Judea, He traveled through Samaria and stopped in a town called Sychar, which was near the property Jacob gave to his son Joseph. Normally, Jewish travelers went around Samaria to avoid contact with the Samaritans, but Jesus didn't. He took the route straight from the south to the north. Taking a path few others took meant meeting people few others met. As a result, there was a divine appointment prepared for Him, and that divine appointment led to revival in a city.

Pause for a moment. Look over your notes. What stood out to you from this video teaching?

Have you ever had an unexpected encounter with someone after taking an unexpected route? If so, describe it.

Have you ever been at the point of exhaustion, feeling like you had nothing left to give, and someone turned up who needed help? What did you do?

What barriers did Jesus break in order to have this conversation?

Why did Jesus start the conversation by talking about water? What can we learn from this as it relates to our own encounters with people who need Jesus, even when we may be tired?

If we are going to reach people, then we have to go where people are. Besides church, what are some places you go often? Do you have opportunities to have spiritual conversations at these places?

Do you really believe Jesus is the only hope for people who are hurting, lost, broken, and hopeless? Is that belief reflected in your words and actions? Explain.

When was the last time you told someone your story of how you came to know Jesus?

Despite what her community had done to her, the Samaritan woman gave them the greatest gift she could—the story of how living water changed her life. She told her story! Authentic. Real. Raw. And compelling, because they knew her. Because she had been with Jesus, she had to go talk about Jesus. That's when the people came to hear Jesus for themselves. That's when they, too, went from being lost to being found.

What about you? You have a story to tell as well, and there is a community longing to hear it. There is a revival waiting to happen.

## MOVE

Review the list of places you go often. Pray for a divine encounter with someone you would not normally interact with in one of these places.

Do you already know someone who needs to hear your story? Who is it? What steps will you take this week to tell your story to this person?

## PRAY

Heavenly Father, help me to share with others the greatest gift You have given to me—living water. Thank You for freeing me from my shame. Help me learn to tell the story of what You have done in my life and spread the good news of the gospel.

# DAY 1
## *WOMEN AREN'T GOD'S PLAN B*

I was mesmerized as I listened to Carol share her story of how Jesus radically changed her life. She was a biker, addicted to drugs and dropping acid, when Jesus got her attention. Since I was only fourteen at the time, I wasn't entirely sure what acid was, but I could tell it was something to steer away from. From what she described, I deduced that hallucinations weren't a good thing—even if you did think you saw Jesus in the midst of them.

Carol was saved in the late 70s, the era of the Jesus movement and coffee shop revivals. But now she was just another one of the mums who helped out at my school. It was the 1980s, and religious education was a compulsory requirement in Australia's public school system. Carol's passionate relationship with Jesus and our school's need for religion teachers intersected, and that's when her life bumped into mine.

Every Tuesday, she taught us what she knew about Jesus. Some kids were bored and even slept through the class, but I couldn't keep my eyes off Carol. I was hanging on her every word.

I grew up in a very formal church. I knew who Jesus was; in fact, He was gloriously depicted with statues, on stained-glass windows, on prayer cards, and in books. But I had no idea about the Jesus that Carol knew. She seemed to know Him in a way I didn't understand. I couldn't help but be intrigued. And the more she taught, the more I anticipated Tuesdays.

Did you have a Carol in your life? Someone who first whet your appetite for Jesus? Someone who took the time to talk to you about Him? In Paul's second letter to his protégé, Timothy, he wrote, "I recall your sincere faith that first lived in your grandmother Lois and in your mother Eunice and now, I am convinced, is in you also" (2 Tim. 1:5). Lois and Eunice were women like Carol, women who talked about the good news of the gospel.

Think back on your spiritual journey and when you were first awakened to the good news. Was there a Lois, Eunice, or Carol in your life? Did God use a specific woman to guide you during that time? If so, write her name here.

What other women have picked up the baton of faith and influenced your life through the years?

I'm so grateful for the women who have mentored me and shaped me through the years. Key women have helped me learn how to be a better wife, mother, teacher, speaker, writer, and leader. I'm especially grateful for how they taught me to develop my capacity so that I could lead global organizations like A21 and Propel.

Who is your current mentor or spiritual mother that you depend on for wisdom and advice?

God has always valued women and included them in His plans to introduce Jesus to the world. They were never a plan B, but very much a part of His master plan from the beginning. From Genesis forward, God has called upon women. In the Old Testament, they were instrumental in the following ways:

- Eve was called the mother of all the living (Gen. 3:20).
- Sarah was called the mother of nations (Gen. 17:15-16, NIV).
- Rahab hid the Israelite spies in Jericho (Josh. 2).
- Deborah judged the people rightly and helped lead the Israelite army to victory over the Canaanites (Judg. 4).
- Ruth was David's great-grandmother (Ruth 4:13-17).
- Esther saved the Jewish people from annihilation (the Book of Esther).

God used all these women to protect the lineage of Jesus—the Savior who was to come. Then, when it was time for Jesus to enter the earth, God included women in His plan again.

- He chose a Mary, a young virgin from Nazareth, to miraculously carry and give birth to the Messiah (Luke 1–2).
- He opened the womb of Elizabeth, who was far past child-bearing years, to bear the forerunner of Christ, John the Baptist (Luke 1).
- He used Anna, a prophetess, soon after Jesus' birth to proclaim Jesus as the Messiah (Luke 2:36-38).

Jesus didn't ignore women, discard them, or overlook them during His earthly ministry.

Look up the following verses and note the women Jesus interacted with. Take note of when He spoke to women in a day when men didn't speak directly to women other than their wives or daughters.[53]

Matthew 8:14-15

Mark 5:35-42

Luke 8:43-48

John 12:1-3

Did you know that during the days of Jesus' earthly ministry, a group of women traveled with Him and supported Him out of their own resources? Imagine their impact on other women in the communities where Jesus traveled.

Look up Luke 8:1-3 and list the women who traveled with Jesus.

Joanna, the wife of Chuza, the manager of Herod's household, was out traveling with Jesus, supporting Him out of her own means, while her husband was running the king's court. In a culture where women had no rights, were seen as property, and rarely had their own resources, this was incredible! In an age when women were usually very limited due to their social status, Jesus included them on His evangelistic itinerant ministry team.

To this day, in many cultures women are overlooked, devalued, and subjected to injustice. I see this on a daily basis through my work with A21 across the globe. Nonetheless, God has never—nor will He ever—dismissed women. God has always loved, esteemed, valued, and included women in His mission.

Many women were at Jesus' crucifixion, including His own mother, Mary, and her sister, and the women who followed Jesus from Galilee—Mary the wife of Clopas, Mary Magdalene, and Mary the mother of James, Joseph, and Salome (Matt. 27:55; Mark 15:40-41; Luke 23:27-30,49; John 19:25).

> Women were the first at the empty tomb, the first to see Jesus, the first entrusted with the linchpin of our Christian faith, "He is risen. He is not here," and the first to go and tell others. Review the following passages and answer the questions below.
>
> Mark 16:1-9
>
> Luke 24:1-10
>
> John 20:11-18

Which women were at the tomb?

What did Jesus say to them to comfort them?

What did Jesus tell the women to go and do?

Why do you think Jesus first appeared to women after His resurrection?

Could it be that Jesus knew a woman could spread news like no one else? After His resurrection, we see in Scripture a great host of women involved in spreading the gospel when the church was birthed.

Look up the following verses and note how many and what kind of women were involved in spreading the gospel through the work of the early church.

**Acts 16:11-15,40**

**Acts 17:4**

**Acts 17:12**

**Romans 16:3,9,12**

I love the fact that God does not choose one particular type of woman for His mission but every type. From the pages of Scripture we see that He used single and married women, educated and uneducated women, homemakers and businesswomen, mothers and scarred women. The good news is we all get to play our part in advancing the mission of God on this earth.

What women in your church or community have been on mission, spearheading the spreading of the gospel? Write about their efforts.

How have you been involved in spreading the gospel in your sphere of influence? How can you currently be involved?

As God nudges you to be involved, go for it. Don't ever think you're not qualified enough, smart enough, or educated enough. You are more than enough for everything God has purposed you to do!

Carol didn't let the lack of a seminary degree stop her from teaching me. What mattered was she knew Jesus and she talked about Him. What mattered was Jesus included her in my journey. When I reconnected with her a few years ago, she was blown away to learn that several of us from class had gone on to spread the good news she'd shared with us. She was overwhelmed with joy to learn what a critical part she played in Jesus' mission to save a handful of school kids and send them to share the gospel with so many others.

God wants us to see ourselves as a critical part of His mission. The women of the Bible saw themselves in this way, and what a difference they made! When I think of the magnitude of their influence, I'm moved to say and do more.

*We are a critical part of God's mission.*

What about you? Do you see yourself as a critical part of Jesus' mission? Do you want to do more? Say more?

I am so thrilled you are doing *this* Bible study at *this* moment. My prayer is that you will discover you are part of a long line of women God has included in His mission on this earth. No one can tell your story like you.

Go and tell. It's what Jesus said to Mary at the tomb (John 20:17). It's what He's commissioned us to do.

# DAY 2

## *GET YOUR GOSSIP ON!*

I grew up in a big, loud Greek family that was anything but boring. Every family gathering included aunts, uncles, and loads of cousins. We always had lots and lots of food—falafel, baklava, moussaka, taramosalata, spanakopita—and always more than we could eat. We celebrated everyone's birthday and anniversary, every holiday and church holy day, and every birth, baptism, and graduation. If there was even the slightest reason to come together and throw a party, we did. Complete with dancing. Honestly, we were just like the movie. Yes, *that* movie.

It was chaotic fun every time. While children were running in and out of the house, and adults were eating, dancing, laughing, and pulling pranks on one another, my mother and my aunts—*the* aunts—were always huddled together discussing everyone's lives. There was nothing worse than overhearing your name and the ensuing conversation about your "plight" in life.

For years, my "plight" was that I wasn't married. When I chose college over marriage they almost never got over it. By their standards, I had to get married so I wouldn't become an old maid and someone to be pitied. When I finally married Nick at thirty, they were thrilled, but then it was a matter of when we were going to have children.

What I remember most about all the aunts is just how much they talked! They talked over one another. They interrupted one another. They started new conversations in the middle of ongoing conversations. They never ran out of things to say.

I've read that women, on average, use twenty thousand words a day and men use seven thousand.[54] Thinking about my aunts, I can believe it! Women definitely have the gift of gab. But why is that? Could it be that God has given women the ability to use so many words for a reason?

We were born to talk. So why not use our natural advantage for the spreading of the gospel? Who better to gossip the gospel than us?

Yes, you read that last sentence correctly. I used the words *gossip* and *gospel* in the same breath! And I'm not the first to do so. Michael Green inspired me when he used the phrase in his book, *Evangelism in the Early Church*.[55] I know God says gossip—malicious gossip—is sin. The Word is clear. But I've got a different idea in mind. Before I explain it, let me assure you that we read the same Bible.

Look up the following verses and note what they say about gossip.

Proverbs 16:28

Proverbs 26:20-22

Romans 1:29-30

The word *gossip* originated in Old English as *godsibb*. *Sibb* was the word for a relative—*godsibb* meant God-parent. In Middle English, it came to refer to idle chatter with any familiar acquaintance—chit-chat with someone you were comfortable with; informal conversation about daily affairs. Now it has the negative connotations that have become predominant today, but in its best and original form, gossip is the familiar, informal conversation between friends.[56]

Women have a knack for being relational, stepping into conversations easily, knowing how to nurture with our words, and simply saying what needs to be said. So why not gossip the gospel? It seems to me we are the perfect secret weapons to spreading the good news.

The secret to gossiping—and it not being sin—is choosing the right words when we speak. Words that heal, not hurt. As much as I tried to pretend I didn't hear my aunts, I heard them loud and clear—and so did everyone else in our family. I loved them and I knew they meant well, but their words hurt.

Words have power—creative power. Gossip is destructive because it uses words to tear down. But what if we turned gossip around and used words to build up?

When God created the world He spoke constructive words. He used them to build the universe. Look up Genesis 1:1-26. In your Bible, underline or note every time you see the words, "Then God said ..."

How many of these phrases did you underline? List all God created just by speaking.

God created the world with words.

> By faith we understand that the universe was created by the word of God, so that what is seen was made from things that are not visible.
> **HEBREWS 11:3**

Looking back at Genesis 1, take special notice of verse 26: "Then God said, 'Let us make man in our image, according to our likeness.'"

God framed the world with words, and by making us in His image, He gave us the power to inspire, design, and build our worlds with words. With our words we can build a bridge for people to come to Christ so their lives will be transformed. We can affirm others, encourage them, build them up, and love them—all with words. We can gossip the gospel to them, can't we?

But we have a choice. As I pointed out earlier, our words can hurt. They have the power to destroy, to demoralize, to discourage, and to dissuade. God wants us to speak words of life every time we speak. He wants us to be conscious of the power of our words the moment we open our mouths.

Look up the following verses and note what they say about the power of our words.

**Proverbs 12:18**

**Proverbs 12:22**

Proverbs 21:23

Ephesians 4:29

Philippians 2:14-15

When have someone's words shattered you? Describe that experience.

When have someone's words built you up and given you the courage to move forward in your life? Describe that experience.

When I think about the power of words, I can't help but wonder: Why not take the same energy it requires to tear down and instead build up? Why not ditch negativity and instead speak words that instill value, encourage success, and communicate confidence? Why not gossip words that bring healing, wisdom, and renewed vision?

Words are also indicators. They reveal our character and what's in our hearts.

Read Matthew 12:33-37 and summarize Jesus' teaching.

Jesus said, "The mouth speaks from the overflow of the heart." Words that may seem trivial or casual can often reflect the true nature of our hearts. Jesus said we will be held accountable for every "careless word" we speak (v. 36). Especially and eternally important are the words we speak about Him (Matt. 10:32-33).

What words are you speaking to Jesus? About Jesus?

With our words we have the power to give our lives fully to God—to confess that Jesus is Lord. Personalize Romans 10:9-10 in the space provided below.

With our words we have the power to praise and glorify God. Personalize Hebrews 13:15 and Colossians 3:16 in the space provided below.

With our words we have the power to gossip the gospel. Personalize 1 Peter 3:15-16a and Colossians 4:6 in the space provided below.

We can literally change the world in which we live, all by influencing one life at a time with the words we speak. God has given women the gift of gab to be used for His glory—to gossip His gospel. We are His secret weapons.

Let's proclaim His good news everywhere we go.

# DAY 3

## *YOU HAVE A STORY TO TELL*

"Mummy, do you think God can use someone like me? I'm not like you. I don't have a big dramatic past or exciting salvation story. My life is pretty normal. Is it possible to make a difference in the world if I don't have a powerful testimony?"

When Catherine asked me that question it rattled me to my core. She had just returned from a week of church camp where a compelling youth evangelist shared his amazing testimony—his history of being lost and found, of being strung out on drugs, addicted to alcohol, wandering in darkness before stepping into the light of Christ—all in hopes of inspiring teens to put their hope in Jesus. I have been the speaker at camps like this countless times for more than three decades, so I completely understood the purpose of his message. But it left Catherine with the idea that because she didn't have a testimony that included a broken past filled with pain, then she didn't really have much to say about her Christian faith and she couldn't be an effective witness.

As a mother, it was sobering to realize I had missed communicating to Catherine the true meaning of the gospel. She had been in church all her life but didn't really understand the heart of the good news of Jesus.

The more I understood Catherine's perspective, the more I couldn't help but think of all the women who have grown up just like her—those who were raised in Christian families, accepted Jesus as Savior as children, and attended church all of their lives. Because of the grace of God, a strong family support system, a positive peer group, and mostly good decisions, many of these women managed to avoid circumstances that caused major trauma. I found myself wondering if they felt like Catherine, like they had nothing to say to a lost and broken world.

To help Catherine realize her own incredible testimony, I knew I had to share with her the good news of the gospel. What she was hearing countless leaders say, in so many words, was that if you had a really bad past, you needed Jesus. But if you didn't have a really bad past, you didn't need Him—or at least not as much.

Nothing could be further from the truth, but that was the point: she didn't fully understand the truth. As I began formulating my thoughts, thinking of where to begin, it occurred to me that before any of us can grasp the good news, we need to comprehend the bad. The bad news is that before I was alive in Christ, I was dead. We all were.

### news

1. newly received or noteworthy information, especially about recent or important events.

2. a broadcast or published report of news.[57]

As Catherine and I began to talk, I explained how Jesus came to make dead people alive, not bad people good. We were all dead upon arrival, and Jesus came to give us new life. And yet, we seem to easily connect to the idea that "I did a bad thing, so I need forgiveness" rather than "There's none righteous, not one, including myself—whether I did a bad thing or not."

I walked Catherine through the Word—the only source of absolute truth—to help her understand the gospel. To help her realize she has a story to tell because the gospel isn't about our behavior or works; it's about Jesus' grace. It's about what He did for us.

> What about you? Could you walk someone through the truth of the gospel? Look up the following passages, and, using them as a basis, write an explanation of the gospel.
>
> **Romans 3:21-26; 5:6-11; 10:9-10,13**
>
> **1 Corinthians 15:1-4**
>
> **Ephesians 2:1-10**

The truth is we are all sinners, born into sin. We were all spiritually dead, separated from God. And the punishment for our sin is death, eternal death. We have no power within ourselves to rectify this grave situation. But God took the initiative. Out of His love for us, He reconciled us to Himself by sending Jesus to be the sinless sacrifice on our behalf. Through Christ's death and resurrection, sin is atoned for, death is defeated, and abundant and eternal life is made available to us. It's a free gift we can receive through repentance of our sins and faith in the finished work of Christ. There is no salvation apart from personal faith in Jesus Christ as Lord. It is by grace we are saved.

This free gift of salvation ensures we are alive in Christ and that our home will be in heaven after we die, but it also allows us to experience His abundant life here on earth and then share that abundant life with others.

Read John 10:10. What does having life in abundance mean to you?

The word "life" in this verse is the Greek word *zoe*, which means "the absolute fulness of life, both essential and ethical, which belongs to God" and "life real and genuine, a life active and vigorous, devoted to God, blessed."[58]

When I explained this to Catherine, she immediately thought of our churches in Thessaloniki, Sofia, and Warsaw—all named Zoe Church, because Jesus wants us to live that kind of life here. Remember, the gospel is about going from death to life. Some of us are so relieved we're going to heaven when we die we forget to live *zoe* life—life real and genuine, a life active and vigorous, devoted to God, blessed—right here on earth.

Can you imagine what kind of witness we would be if we exhibited a radiant life? Not a trouble-free life, but an abundant life. Not a pain-free life, but an abundant life. Not an easy life, but an abundant life.

If the sole purpose of salvation is to go to heaven when we die, then wouldn't it be more merciful of Jesus if, after He saved us, He took us home immediately? But we have a purpose to fulfill here on earth. We are the sent ones commissioned to go into all the world and proclaim His good news.

Sometimes I think we feel more pressure to share about how to live a moral life than how to live an abundant life. Could it be that our testimony would mean more if we shared about the abundant life God has given us?

I meet moral people all the time—people who are good and want to do good—but they still need Jesus to be saved and have an abundant life. They have to be born again.

Read John 3:1-21 and write what Jesus said about being born again.

Write about when you first gave your heart to Jesus and what He did for you.

If you found that you couldn't write your testimony because you've never surrendered your life to Christ, I encourage you to pray right now and ask Jesus to be the Lord of your life. You can do that by expressing repentance and faith through a prayer such as this:

*Heavenly Father, I repent of my sins and ask You to forgive me. I invite Jesus into my heart to be the Lord of my life. I give You all of me. In Jesus' name I pray. Amen.*

*The gospel is about going from death to life.*

The power of salvation is in what Jesus did for us because He loves us. We were dead and He made us alive. He gave us abundant life. Therefore, we have equally powerful stories—because all of our stories are actually the same story. And it's time to go and tell it.

Look up the following verses that tell why it is important for you to share your story.

Romans 1:16

Romans 10:14-15

1 Peter 3:15

God wants you to use your voice where you are—where you shop, dine, work, worship, serve, exercise, and play. He has called you to influence your world. Share the gospel. Tell your story!

# DAY 4

## *THE JOY OF OUR SALVATION*

"Chris, you have cancer." Those will forever be some of the most shocking words I have ever heard.

I felt a lump on the side of my neck, but I never imagined it would be something so serious. My doctor told me I had four separate conditions: a growth on the left side of my throat, nodules on my vocal chords, a throat infection, and thyroid cancer.

To my doctor's surprise—and to God's glory—more tests a couple weeks later revealed the nodules were gone. It was miraculous. The rest required medication for a period of time and two different surgeries, but no chemo or radiation. I was so relieved when, three months later, I was declared cancer-free.

But on the heels of that experience, a series of heartbreaks hammered away at me, beginning with my mum's death. Although she was ailing at the time, my brothers and I thought we had several more months before we would have to say goodbye. Six weeks after her funeral, my sister-in-law, who had been a part of my life longer than Nick and I had been married, passed away as well. Then, we lost two of Nick's family members. It was like the hits just kept coming.

The final blow was when a dear friend whom I loved wholeheartedly suddenly cut me off. Without warning. Without explanation.

We eventually did speak, but only after weeks of racking my brain trying to figure out what I'd done wrong. And all of this happened while I continued to travel, speak, write, and lead our ministry teams.

The losses in that season of my life stacked up faster than I could process them. Faster than my heart could grieve and off-load them. Before I knew it, I found myself in a place I'd never been before—and never intended to go. I felt no excitement about my future. I pulled back from people close to me. I found myself closing off my heart so I would never be hurt like that again. I was going through the motions of spiritual disciplines, but my prayers had grown stale and my Bible reading felt more obligatory than anticipatory.

Nick really got my attention the day he said, "Chris, your spark is missing. What's wrong?"

That's when I took it to God. I realized I had allowed the disappointments to begin robbing me of the joy of my salvation.

Realizing I was in danger of losing my joy, which is rooted in God, was both shocking and gut-wrenching. Shocking because I thought I was stronger than that. Gut-wrenching because facing the truth meant facing *more* truth.

It was also sobering. I knew that losing the joy of my salvation would affect my eagerness to go and tell the good news, something I never wanted to let slip.

When I stopped long enough to be quiet, to figure out how I'd gotten to this unexpected place, I knew I had to start right where I was—disappointed, hurt, and discouraged—and grieve my losses. I had to face the truth in my heart that I felt forgotten by God. Of course, I knew from the Scripture He would never leave me nor forsake me, but there was a fight to be won between my head and my heart. Because of my background of abandonment and abuse, I can feel rejection and abandonment deeply, sometimes confusing what people do to me as something God does. All the losses in that short period of time triggered deep pain, and I felt exposed and vulnerable. I was surprised to realize how subtle and easy it is to tuck away an offense toward God in the corner of my heart, but I had to be completely honest—with myself and with God.

Admitting all this was the first step toward my healing. God wasn't shocked by all my wrestling; He was the One who helped me recognize what was going on because He wanted to heal me.

I had to stop many of the activities I was doing for God so I could reconnect intimately with Him. During that season, I kept coming back to David's prayer: "Restore the joy of your salvation to me, and sustain me by giving me a willing spirit" (Ps. 51:12).

> Think back to the joy you experienced when you were saved. What do you recall about that day?

When we sense the joy of our salvation start to slip away, God wants us to be honest and transparent, just as David was in Psalm 51. David lost the joy of God's salvation because of his sin. Perhaps that's your experience. Or perhaps you're like me, and your joy slipped away because of hits that kept coming. Regardless, God wants us to be honest and transparent. Though it's tempting to pretend, we can't deny what we're feeling. We must invite God to heal us and renew our joy, because there are too many other lives at risk—the people God has called us to go and tell about His good news.

Have you walked through a difficult season during which you suffered repeated loss, heartbreak, or tragedy? Describe that time.

How did that season affect you emotionally? Consider the list below and check any emotions you felt.
☐ Abandonment
☐ Anger
☐ Anxiety
☐ Apathy
☐ Depression
☐ Disappointment
☐ Discouragement
☐ Disillusionment
☐ Doubt
☐ Fear
☐ Loneliness
☐ Rejection
☐ Resentment
☐ Sadness
☐ Weariness
☐ Other:_____

How did that season affect your spiritual life? Did you feel the joy of your salvation begin to slip away? Did you feel like God had abandoned you or was ignoring you? Explain.

Where are you now? If you're still struggling, ask God to restore your joy. And keep asking until He does. He who promised is faithful (Heb. 10:23).

In the Hebrew, the word "restore" is *shuwb*. It means "to return, refresh, repair."[59] That was exactly what I needed God to do for me: repair and renew the joy of His salvation within in me.

## re·store

1. bring back (a previous right, practice, custom, or situation); reinstate.

2. return (someone or something) to a former condition, place, or position.

3. repair or renovate (a building, work of art, vehicle, etc.) so as to return it to its original condition.[60]

When I prayed for God to restore my joy, He walked me through more of His Word and showed me the way forward. It was an incredible journey that I want to share with you. To start, we'll deepen our understanding of joy, and then examine how joy connects to our salvation and telling the good news.

First, read the following passages and note what each writer says about salvation.

Hebrews 2:1-4

1 Peter 1:8-9

The writer of Hebrews said we should not neglect "such a great salvation," and Peter said we should rejoice with "inexpressible and glorious joy" over this great salvation.

Joy comes from our relationship with God, but where specifically? Look up the following verses to find the answer.

Romans 14:17

Galatians 5:22-23

1 Thessalonians 1:6

Our joy comes from the One Jesus sent to help us spread the gospel—the Holy Spirit, who lives inside us.

> Joy is a powerful emotion, a natural response to the goodness of God in our lives and so great a salvation! Look up the following verses and write what else you discover about joy.

> Nehemiah 8:10

> Psalm 30:1-5

> John 15:10-11

> Psalm 16:11

You and I do not have the natural strength to fight all the battles that come into our lives. We need God's strength to live in His victory—and that strength comes from spending time in His presence. The joy of our salvation is found in Him, and the fullness of joy is found in His presence.

Think back to this week's video teaching. Remember the woman at the well? That long conversation represents great intimacy with Jesus. Out of that intimacy came her joy and excitement to go and tell her community about Jesus. Like the woman, our talking about Jesus comes out of our intimacy with Him, out of our remaining in Him (John 15:5). Before we can have joy and spread the good news of the gospel, we first need to be with Jesus. To be renewed by Him. To be refreshed and restored. To talk to Him. If we talk to Jesus, we can't help but want to talk about Jesus!

*We need God's strength to live in His victory.*

## DAY 5

### *STRIKE THE RIGHT TONE*

"Chris, it's not what you say; it's how you say it!"

Those words stung because they weren't the first time I'd heard them. Nick and I were at an impasse, trying to resolve a conflict that needed a solution. But somehow, we'd gotten off track from making a decision and onto a discussion about how we were communicating.

When I expressed that I felt like Nick wasn't hearing me, his response stopped me in my tracks. Though it was rough to hear, I got it. Even after all the changing I've done over the decades, I'm still only human. And sometimes my "get it done" personality can overtake my heart's intent to be softer.

What about you? Has anyone ever said to you, "It's not what you say; it's how you say it"? It's easy to talk without realizing how we sound until suddenly we recognize the person we're speaking to isn't listening anymore.

> When was the last time you said something to your husband, kids, friends, or coworkers and you could tell they stopped listening to you?

> Why do you think they quit listening? Was there a difference between how you intended to speak and how you actually spoke? Explain.

The tone in a conversation can be the difference between whether people receive what we're saying or not. Tone can be defined as an "accent or inflection of the voice as adapted to the emotion or passion expressed."[61] It exposes our insincerity or affirms our trustworthiness. It's what makes what we're saying attractive and engaging—or offensive and unappealing. Tone is a critical component in our communication.

Why do parents say things like, "I don't like your tone" or "Don't you take that tone with me"? What makes tone such an issue?

What about a coworker's email WRITTEN IN ALL CAPS? How does the tone affect your receptivity?

Tone is powerful. It's important when it comes to the way we speak, especially if we want to
be heard.

King Solomon penned some tone comparisons in the Bible. Look up the following verses and note how tone makes a difference.

**Proverbs 15:1-2**

**Proverbs 15:4**

**Proverbs 16:24**

**Proverbs 25:11-12**

**Proverbs 25:15**

We've established this week that God made us to talk—He gave us the gift of gab to spread the gospel—but if we're communicating in such a way that people aren't listening, then how are we impacting lives? Just because we are *telling* the good news doesn't guarantee that people are *hearing* the good news.

Jesus knew how to speak to people so He was heard.

Read Luke 4:22 and write what His hometown friends said about His tone below.

Jesus spoke with a gracious tone, and it affected how the people who knew Him heard Him.

Just last year, I joined a new gym and quickly became friends with a woman named Amy.* She was in her late forties, single, focused on her career, and moving up the corporate ladder. She was easy to talk to and full of life. For weeks we worked out alongside one another, encouraging each other and laughing at the stories we exchanged. Over time she began to open up more about her personal life.

She was recently divorced. Her husband left her after she had an affair. Her mother was a "religious nut"—her words, not mine—who had turned her off to church when she was younger. I took that as my first clue to initially talk more about my work with A21 than my involvement with church. I had to keep the door open, waiting for the right moment. Genuine friendship earns us the right to speak into people's lives.

*We have to be winsome if we want to win some.*

Amy knew Nick and I had been married for more than two decades and that we had two daughters we thoroughly enjoyed. One day she wanted to know why, after being married for so long, I wouldn't want to "get out there" and find more variety.

The tone of my answer was as crucial as its content. We have to be winsome if we want to win some, even when faced with the most challenging conversations.

Have you been in a similar situation, knowing that how you said something was going to be just as crucial as what you said? Describe that moment.

I had a choice to make: I could say things that referenced how we're supposed to behave, and make her feel I was passing judgment on her behavior. Or, I could speak in such a way that I met her need to be loved, accepted, and valued. I could use it as an opportunity to make her feel seen and known, like Jesus did for the woman at the well.

So, I chose my tone carefully. I used the opportunity to share my biblical values and my faith in Jesus in a non-judgmental way. I explained how I based my decisions on the Bible. I explained that as a follower of Jesus I believe marriage is a covenant to be kept exclusively between a man and a woman. I shared my heart that I would never want to do anything to jeopardize the love and trust Nick and I share. Then, to keep the conversation from feeling too heavy, I joked: Why would I want to have anyone else when I have the best?

Amy laughed with me, but she was blown away by my perspective. So many of the men she had met online were married and had no issue with having extramarital affairs. She was astounded that Nick and I wouldn't consider it. My answering her so honestly, but tenderly, prompted a dozen more questions. Since then, we've gone out to dinner, continued to work out together, and texted regularly. The right tone cemented our friendship. She hasn't come to faith in Christ yet, but she is open to the gospel. It is amazing how much people love to hear truth when it is full of love, grace, and acceptance.

> When was the last time someone asked you such a probing question—and the answer was clearly grounded in your Christian faith and values? How did you answer? Did your answer keep the door open for future conversations?

Answering people truthfully, but not offensively, is a learning process. We can't control how every person hears us, but we can make sure our tone reflects the tender love and mercy of God. We must rely on the Holy Spirit in every conversation.

> Read Ephesians 4:15. What phrase did Paul use that should be the goal of our conversations? What do you think it means?

I knew it was necessary to tell Amy the truth, even though I knew the truth—God's truth—seems countercultural in today's world. So many people are completely comfortable with the idea of you having your version of the truth and me having mine, and as long as we don't get into each other's faces, we can each believe what we want to. People seem to think their personal preferences are equal to the truth—but nothing could be further from the truth. Paul wrote that we're to speak the truth in love, not throw out truth in the name of love.

> We know from the Bible that truth is absolute because it's founded on a rock-solid foundation. Look up the following verses and describe the two sources of absolute truth.

> John 14:6

> John 17:17

Speaking the truth—absolute truth—is important, but it's equally important to speak it graciously and in love. When we have a gracious tone, people hear the truth in love because we are not deafening them with a tone of judgment, condemnation, and superiority. And sometimes we don't have to give all the truth at once. Sometimes it's better to share some truth one conversation at a time.

Peter wrote that we are to be ready to answer anyone who asks about our hope in Jesus (1 Pet. 3:15). But Peter said tone matters.

> Look up 1 Peter 3:15-16 and write the two words Peter used to describe how we're to answer (v. 16).

For people to hear what we have to say, it matters how we say it. In a world full of outrage and anger over so many issues, may we be the most loving, kind, peaceful, gentle, patient, and full of self-control people anyone has ever met— and may our words convey such a tone.

*While Amy represents a real person I met at the gym, I have given her a fictitious name to protect her privacy.

# BRING GLIMPSES OF HEAVEN TO EARTH

# REFRAME YOUR VIEW

## WATCH

Watch Video Week 6, *Don't Say No When God Says Go*, and record your personal thoughts as you listen.

_____

_____

_____

_____

_____

_____

_____

_____

_____

_____

_____

_____

_____

_____

_____

_____

_____

_____

_____

_____

_____

## DISCUSS

Our God chose us for this time and this place. He is in control, and He has given us all we need to fulfill His purpose in our generation. There is no other plan. You and I are it. We are the ones He has sent to go into all the world and make disciples. Isn't that an astounding thought?

> Pause for a moment. Look over your notes. What stood out to you from the video teaching?

> Are you one who is eager to break camp and move forward or stay where you are and enjoy the comfort? Explain.

> What's the main thing keeping you from breaking camp and moving forward?

> Have you ever thought about how risky life is? Have you taken risks even today?

> What's the riskiest thing you've ever done?

> Would you say we're consumed with being safe? And that this desire to stay safe keeps us from fulfilling God's purpose and advancing His kingdom? Explain.

> Do you have a fear keeping you spiritually paralyzed?

> Does "You have been at this mountain long enough" apply to you? How so?

We weren't created to live safe, comfortable, boring, or predictable lives. We were created, wired, and transformed to be risk-takers—people who live by faith, walk by faith, and go out into our world to share our faith.

## MOVE

What is God asking you to risk? Where is He asking you to go?

What steps will you take to move forward this week? Be specific.

## PRAY

Heavenly Father, thank You that You have seen me, chosen me, and sent me. Help me to have the strength and courage to go where You tell me to go and do what You have called me to do.

# DAY 1

## *BREAKING OUT OF THE BUBBLE*

Growing up as the daughter of first-generation Greek immigrants meant growing up in a very Greek bubble. Before I was born, thousands of Greek immigrants settled in Sydney—and the biggest impact they brought with them was their Greek-ness! Our home—along with plenty others—had more trinkets and statues and tributes to the motherland than you could imagine. If something could be painted, bought, or displayed in blue and white colors, it was. Everything from iconic columns to painted porch furniture to flowerpots saluted Greece.

Because my parents—and all their friends—came to Australia with no one to rely on but each other, they huddled together, firmly entrenched in the idea that there is safety in numbers. Even long after it was necessary. So, during my childhood, everywhere we went was an all-Greek affair—birthday parties, weddings, church. Even if we went on a short holiday, it was with other Greek relatives. My parents and aunts and uncles and cousins and friends and neighbors stayed within this tight-knit Greek community as much as possible.

And it wasn't because they didn't speak English. My parents actually spoke five languages: Arabic, Greek, French, Italian, and English. They were brilliant people. They knew how to navigate modern society, but they chose to live in a small world of their own making.

For my brothers and me, all of this homogenous living was just the way it was. When non-Greek friends invited us over for dinner, to a slumber party, or to a high school dance, our parents rarely allowed us to go. They preferred that we stay in the setting where they felt safe and secure and in control of us. Truthfully, I think they expected us to carry on our Greek heritage as though the rest of Sydney's cultural diversity and influence didn't exist—but that wasn't realistic or healthy.

My brothers and I were Greek, and we loved our Greek heritage, but we were Australians by birth. We wanted to explore our country and all it had to offer. I wanted to venture out and embrace a culture far beyond my own.

I think that sometimes we Christians behave similarly to my parents and their friends. We live in a Christian bubble, inside our Christian communities, inside our collective of Christian friends—and we stay there. Perhaps, we even hide out there. We design what we think is heaven on earth—the perfect religious world—and we hunker down in hopes all will go well until we leave this planet. But Jesus has sent us out into the world to make disciples.

We can't make His last commandment our first priority if we don't break out of our bubble.

I understand that sometimes the bubble just happens. We get saved, we make Christian friends, we grow in Christ, and we naturally enjoy the camaraderie, safety, security, and comfort of our Christian community. But over time, we find ourselves trapped in the bubble, rarely interacting with people who don't look, think, or believe like us. We don't work out with them at the gym, or take them to lunch, or invite them to our homes. And yet, that's exactly what Jesus tells us to do.

Jesus didn't save us to build a Christian subculture. He didn't save us to hide from the world, avoid the world, ignore the world, fear the world, hate the world, condemn the world, or judge the world. He sent us into the world to love the world He created and loves so tenderly and fiercely.

Two sentences of Jesus' model prayer speak of us moving out into the world.

Look up Matthew 6:9-13. Write the prayer in the space provided below. Underline verses 10-11a.

What did Jesus mean when He prayed, "Your kingdom come. Your will be done on earth as it is in heaven" (v. 10)?

The kingdom of God is defined as "the rule of God." The rule of God is God setting things right to make people and the world work as He intended them to work.[62]

## king·dom of God

1. the realm in which God's will is fulfilled.[63]

Jesus prayed for the kingdom to come to earth—not for it to stay in heaven or for us to wait until we get to heaven to participate in it. He taught us to pray the same way. Here is the exciting part: we are the church; therefore, we represent the manifest presence of God in the world. You and me. We are the body of Christ, the hands and feet of Jesus. So we must break out of the bubble and get to work in the world doing His kingdom work, those works "which God prepared ahead of time for us to do" while we're here on earth (Eph. 2:10).

### ZOOM IN

Author Reggie McNeal writes in his book, *Kingdom Come, Why We Must Give Up Our Obsession with Fixing the Church—and What We Must Do Instead*, "Our relationship with God and our human interactions—with ourselves, with one another, with other living beings, and with the planet itself—all fall into the category of the Kingdom. This means that Kingdom concerns extend well beyond what we generally think of as spiritual matters to include culture, art, literature, education, politics, business and economics, the environment—the full range of human enterprise and consequences. If humans are involved in it, the Kingdom of God has a stake in it."[64]

For most of us the concept of a king and kingdom is foreign (except for those of us who are still under a constitutional monarchy). So to understand the kingdom of God we need to remember that a kingdom reflects the character of its king.

Read Psalm 145. List all the attributes of our King according to this passage. Look for words like "greatness," "goodness," and "righteousness." You should be able to find at least a dozen or more.

Part of our bringing glimpses of heaven to earth is reflecting the attributes of our King. Look over your list. Are you currently reflecting those attributes? Explain.

When we bring glimpses of heaven to earth we bring glory to God. Our lives—our character, words, and actions—draw people's attention to Him and His goodness and all the ways He's gracious, merciful, compassionate, and worthy to be trusted.

Too often we want to make the Christian life about our agenda, about what's best for us. That's *not* the kingdom of God.

**Look up Romans 14:17 again and write Paul's definition of the kingdom of God.**

This verse is set in a discussion on Christian liberty—specifically what foods to eat and what foods to abstain from. Paul made it clear we don't live for ourselves, we live for the Lord (Rom. 14:7-8). So, it's His agenda that is most important. Paul concluded, then, that the kingdom of God is not about what food we eat, or what carpet color we choose for the worship center, or whether we sing hymns or choruses. Those are Christian bubble issues, not kingdom issues. The kingdom is about the work of God in us and through us.

God has made us righteous and has given us peace and joy in the Holy Spirit. That same Spirit empowers us to move out into the world.

**Read Acts 1:8 and write it below.**

We need to remember that our salvation is far more than a prayer we prayed. It is far more than the assurance that when we die we will go to heaven. Yes, we have been saved from the penalty of sin through the work of Jesus Christ on the cross, but our story does not end there.

We have been saved not only from something but for something: the work of the kingdom here on earth, the mission of the church.

When Jesus came, He declared the kingdom of God was at hand (Mark 1:14-15) —meaning here, now. And He demonstrated it! He opened blind eyes. He healed deaf ears. He spoke, and those who were crippled walked. He multiplied food. He turned water into wine. He commanded the forces of evil to go … and they went. He even raised the dead. When Jesus came, the kingdom of God broke into the here and now in power.

And when Jesus died and rose again, He secured victory over evil once and for all. He has won. The end of all things has already been written, and we know it.

A day is coming when evil will be brought to an end, suffering and sickness will cease, justice will prevail, and every wrong will be made right once and for all (Rev. 7:16-17; 21:4-8; 22:3-5).

Through Jesus, God's rule has already entered into our here and now, but it is not yet fully realized, as the fullness of His kingdom will not come until Jesus returns. As a result, we're living in a period of "already and not yet." How are we to live in this time?

Not in a holy huddle. Not in a Christian bubble.

We are to move out into the world with the good news of the gospel. Until the time that Jesus' kingdom comes in its fullness, we are to carry His kingdom of hope and healing into a broken world that desperately needs Him. It's the reason we have been seen, chosen, and sent.

# DAY 2

## JUSTICE: MAKING WHAT'S WRONG, RIGHT

Trembling from head to toe, Pensri* sat on the gurney, too terrified to speak. The bruises on her arms and neck said enough. Though she appeared to be barely a teen, it was clear she had been used and violated in unspeakable ways. As the medical team examined her, Katie,* one of our A21 team members, stayed close, holding her hand and stroking her hair.

The police had found Pensri crouched near a dumpster, hiding from everyone but the rats that called the alleyway home. From all appearances, she hadn't been there long, which meant someone was still looking for her. It was urgent they get her to safety. Coaxing her as best they could, promising not to hurt her, they were barely able to gain her trust. When she agreed to go with them, the police called A21 at our office in Pattaya. That's when Katie met the police and took Pensri to the hospital.

In the following weeks, our team supported Pensri with no strings attached and no expectations. The more we served her with a safe place to live, good food to eat, clean clothes to wear, and continued medical care, the more she began to trust us and let down her guard.

From time to time the police checked with our team, hoping Pensri might tell them how she ended up by the dumpster that night. But they knew it wasn't likely to ever happen. She had been trafficked, of that they were certain. They found her in Thailand but she could have been from anywhere in Southeast Asia—Cambodia, Vietnam, Laos. Anywhere.

Still, they hoped.

In the meantime, our team continued to care for her.

One day, to Katie's surprise, Pensri confided that she wanted to tell her story. The risk she was willing to take didn't escape Katie. She knew, as did Pensri, the threat would always exist of being recaptured, never seeing her family again, and sentenced to certain death.

Pensri courageously told her story to a social worker in a room at the Child Advocacy Center—a place built by A21 in conjunction with the Royal Thai Police, the Federal Bureau of Investigation, the U.S. Department of Homeland Security, and the Thai Internet Crimes Against Children—while it was recorded and observed by police and a prosecutor in a separate room. This allowed her to tell her story once in a safe and secure environment, so as not to re-traumatize her.

Because of Pensri's courage, the police were able to identify more than thirty other victims of the same trafficking ring that had held her captive. Multiple arrest warrants were issued. Currently, three traffickers are serving time in jail.

The thirty victims who were rescued have been given access to support and care—just like Pensri was—and reunited with their families.

Pensri has surprised us once more by becoming one of the biggest advocates for women in her local community. To this day, our team meets with her weekly to continue to show her support.

I thank God she is free and justice has been served.

Look up Micah 6:8 and write what God says about justice below.

Depending on your translation, the first command is to act justly. Our broken world is full of injustices, and part of our mandate as sent ones is to address what's wrong and make it right. We are to carry the light of Christ to the broken places and systems in our world.

When we see injustice on the earth and proactively choose to do something about it, people notice, and it brings glory to God. When people see that we see them and choose to get involved to make wrong things right, they will be more open to a God who cares deeply about them.

### jus·tice
1.  the quality of being just; righteousness, equitableness, or moral rightness.[65]

Look up the following verses and write what else you discover about God and justice.

Psalm 33:5

Psalm 106:3

Proverbs 21:15

Isaiah 51:4-5

Isaiah 61:8-9

Jeremiah 22:3

Luke 18:1-8

You'll notice most of these verses show us that God is a God of justice—He loves justice and brings about justice. The words for justice in the Bible (*tsedeq* and *mishpat*, and the Greek word *dikaiosyne*) are interchangeable with righteousness.[66]

Our salvation impacts every sphere of our lives. Because of that, followers of Jesus should be disturbed whenever we see poverty, prejudice, inequality, ageism, racism, misogyny, coverups of abuse, unemployment, or a lack of access to education or healthcare. If it is in our power to do something, then we should. We have been sent into this world to show evidences of the fullness of God's kingdom to come, when all things will be made new, and part of that mandate is to help make wrong things right.

I understand how overwhelming this can be. When we think of the magnitude of pain and injustice on the earth, it's normal to think we can't do anything to make a real difference. We look at our lack of knowledge, skills, resources, power, understanding, or authority and become paralyzed. I know how frustrating it is to see a problem and feel there isn't anything to do to help. There are times I feel this way about the work of A21.

There are tens of millions of victims of modern-day slavery scattered around the world today. And to think, until I saw the posters of missing women and girls, I had no idea this was going on around me in virtually every city I visited—in the United States, in Europe, and all the way around the world.

In the beginning, the more I learned about human trafficking, the more I felt like giving up. But I reminded myself that God has called me to see the *one*. If I kept seeing the *one*, I could keep myself going.

Where to start? Prayer. Begin by asking God to break your heart for what breaks His. Ask Him to show you where you can get involved in the fight for justice. Feel free to write your prayer below.

I've also found that knowledge is invaluable. Before we launched A21, we conducted loads of research. It's hard to pray for something you know nothing about. It is hard to do something about something you know nothing about.

List some of the major injustices on the earth today, and then dive into some research of your own.

In Luke 4:18, Jesus, in His first public sermon, said,

The Spirit of the Lord is on me, because he has anointed me to preach good news to the poor. He has sent me to proclaim release to the captives and recovery of sight to the blind, to set free the oppressed.

Did you catch that? Jesus Himself said that there was a reason the Spirit of the Lord was upon Him. There was a *because*. I want to remind you, my sister, there is a *because* aspect to our life of faith.

Look up Romans 8:11 and record what you discover about the Spirit of the Lord.

Look back at Luke 4:18. Underline the five things Jesus said He was sent to do. Circle the four types of people who were the recipients of His ministry. Then identify who those people are in your community—both physically and spiritually.

Jesus was sent to proclaim good news to the poor, to bring liberty to the captives, to give sight to the blind, to set free the oppressed, and to proclaim the favorable year of the Lord. And so are we.

Luke 4:18 makes it clear the gospel has implications for not only those who are lost and need to be found but also the vulnerable who need to be rescued from their oppression.[67]

Read John 20:21 and write it in the space provided below.

As Jesus was sent, we are sent. The same Spirit of the Lord is on us and in us, and we are sent to the same kinds of people.

This is what keeps me going with A21. Every time light wins over darkness, life triumphs over death. Once we know something, we can never unknow it. Once we see something, we can never unsee it. That is true globally, that is true locally, and that is true in our closest relationships. Justice demands that we not only know but also do something about it.

*Though the writing of this story is based on facts, Pensri and Katie are not the women's real names. Their names and surrounding circumstances have been creatively changed to protect their identities.

# DAY 3

## *WE ARE THE HANDS AND FEET OF JESUS*

Walking toward what looked like a demolition site with tall mounds of rubble, I was amazed to see people begin to stand up on top of it all. As I got closer to them I realized they were standing around makeshift campfires to stay warm.

Among the crowd I spied a young girl who looked as cold and helpless as she must have felt. We made eye contact, and I could tell she wanted to speak to me. She carefully worked her way down through broken slabs of concrete and mangled rebar. Once she reached the ground, I saw she was balancing a tiny bundle in her arms.

Meeting her halfway, I smiled into her eyes all the courage and comfort I could, and then I looked more closely at her bundle. It was a newborn baby boy, no more than two or three weeks old.

Her name was Donka.* His name was Farold.* They were part of a community of Romani people, commonly known as Roma Gypsies, who lived in Sofia, Bulgaria, where we have one of our A21 offices and where we work with a local church, Zoe Sofia. I have long loved the Bulgarian people for their resilience and tenacity. That day, I was meeting this community of people whose homes had been bulldozed by the local government. With nowhere else to go, they camped out on top of the rubble of what were once their homes.

Originally from the Punjab region of northern India, the Roma Gypsies are a nomadic people and have traditionally been scorned and persecuted.[68]

Today, Gypsies mostly live in Europe and America. In Sofia, they live in their own community in impoverished conditions—in one of the poorest nations in the European Union. For the past six years, Zoe Sofia has helped serve the Gypsies in Sofia.

When I asked Donka about her son, I was heartbroken to learn that, in addition to all the obvious hardships he faced, he was born HIV positive—something treatable with modern medicine, but on that rubble heap access to modern medicine wasn't likely. Donka and her community had no homes, no sanitation, no water, no electricity—and the dead of winter was yet to come.

I was overwhelmed by their plight and knew we had to do something. As I looked across the piles of rubble and makeshift camps, I thought of the words from Isaiah 58.

Read Isaiah 58:6-12.

Israel was a great nation that triumphed in battle, prospered, and flourished. But despite her faithfulness to religious practices, God's people were not practicing justice. Let's unpack this passage to better understand what God wants us to do when we see those less fortunate.

Reread verses 6-7 and list what Isaiah described as the desired outcome of the fast.

In verses 9-11, Isaiah spoke several if/then clauses. List them here, writing the "if" phrases on the left and the "then" phrases on the right.

| IF | THEN |
| --- | --- |
|  |  |

God doesn't want only our personal religious practices; He wants our investment in breaking the chains that imprison others. The people wanted God's blessing, but to receive His blessing they needed to change their hearts and actions.

When you think about your family, the people living on your street, and your coworkers or fellow students, who needs help that you can provide or orchestrate?

When you consider the outreach ministries of your local church or ministries in your city, where can you get involved to make a difference in the lives of those less fortunate? Write your ideas below.

If you don't know how your church ministers in your community, go find out. If current ministries don't exist, maybe you're the one to spearhead a new one or to help involve people from your church with another local ministry.

When you look around your community, whom do you identify as the poor and the marginalized?

- Is it the adult who never had the chance to learn to read?
- Is it the woman recently released from prison?
- Is it the child in need of a foster home?
- Is it the children who go to bed hungry every night?
- Is the widow who can't afford a new roof for her home?
- Is it the girl with the unexpected pregnancy who doesn't know where to turn for help?

    Do some research on the groups, ministries, and NGOs (non-government organizations) working in your area to reach people who need help. Make a list of opportunities where you can get involved. Then ask God how you can help people in your community.

To better understand why this passage from Isaiah 58 came to mind when I saw the heaps of rubble in Bulgaria, look how verse 12 is worded in The Message:

> You'll be known as those who can fix anything, restore old ruins, rebuild and renovate, make the community livable again.

The beauty of the phrase "make the community livable again" captivated my heart.

No matter how painful it is or how hard it seems, we have been sent into this world to look with the eyes of Jesus, to be moved with the heart of Jesus, and to be the hands and feet of Jesus wherever there is need.

Together with Zoe Sofia church, we started a restoration plan to make the Roma Gypsy community livable. When we found land to buy and planned the construction process, people had hope in their eyes again. They were overwhelmed with gratitude when the children were given access to education and training. It will take time to get everything accomplished, but the process of transformation has begun. Everything starts with doing the next right thing.

When I reflect on what God has called us to do for the Roma Gypsies in Bulgaria, which is still a work in progress, I can't help but think of James 2:14-18.

Read James 2:14-18 and write verses 15-16 below.

Our faith is expressed through our works. We are Jesus' hands and feet to our world! There is something that happens in our hearts when we step into the lives of the vulnerable, when we reach out …

- instead of driving past the homeless person resting on a bench;
- instead of ignoring the person begging at an intersection;
- instead of avoiding the elderly neighbor who is struggling;
- instead of judging the teen mom working at the grocery store;
- instead of neglecting the poor communities in our cities;
- instead of overlooking youth who are at risk and vulnerable.

God's love and mercy for those in need is endless, and He wants to express His love and mercy through us. Look up the following verses and note how reaching out to the needy honors God.

Proverbs 14:31

Proverbs 19:17

Acts 20:35

I'm not asking you to give to the people in Bulgaria, but I am encouraging you to ask God where you can give and get involved.

When I see news of tragedies, political unrest, economic instability, or children going to bed hungry, I have a choice—and so do you. We can look away, or we can pray and ask God, *What can I do?*

When I was standing in front of the rubble heaps in Bulgaria, I could have easily comforted Donka, prayed for her baby, and walked away, leaving it all to the local pastors. I could have retreated to the warmth and comfort of my home in California. But Donka and the others living with her are people created in the image of God, deserving of our compassion and justice. They are people who want the same things I do—love, security, hope, a future, and peace. How can I not at least ask God what I can do to help?

When we reach out to others, God remembers. He sees when we administer His justice and bring a glimpse of heaven to earth. Look up the following verses and summarize what God promises to us when we reach out to those He loves.

Luke 14:13-14

Isaiah 58:9-11

God will be faithful to help us help the ones He puts in our line of sight.

*Though the writing of this story is based on facts, Donka and Farold are not their real names. Their names and surrounding circumstances have been creatively changed to protect their identities.

# DAY 4
## TURN DOWN THE MUSIC

Almost a year before God began to awaken me to the modern-day atrocities of human trafficking—and several months before I saw the posters of missing women and children on the wall in the airport in Thessaloniki—I visited the Auschwitz death camp in Poland.

A friend went with me, and we were both equally horrified to see firsthand the consequences of people ignoring the pain and suffering of others. I remember standing in front of a display of thousands and thousands of shoes, and all I could do was weep. My friend and I were both so impacted that neither of us could speak. I left Auschwitz with a powerful and unshakable conviction that I could no longer sit on the sidelines of humanity's sufferings and injustices.

I remember looking toward heaven that day and whispering a prayer: *God, help me not to close my eyes to other people's horror or ignore injustice. Help me fight the injustice You hate. Help me value people and speak up for those who have been silenced. God, You have loved, chosen, and healed me, and I want to help others be set free. If anything—anything!—like this happens in my lifetime, help me not to sit back and pretend it does not concern me.*[70]

God heard my prayer—and He took my willingness to act seriously. Months later, He called me to start A21. I had no idea where to begin or how to start. It was an overwhelming assignment, and it still is. But I realized I couldn't sit back and do nothing just because I couldn't figure out how to do everything.

There's a sobering story I want to share with you, because it's one that makes this point clear. It's from Erwin Lutzer's book, *When a Nation Forgets God*, and it's a firsthand account from a person who lived in Germany during the 1930s and 1940s when people were being transported to the death camps:

> I lived in Germany during the Nazi Holocaust. I considered myself a Christian. We heard stories of what was happening to the Jews, but we tried to distance ourselves from it because, what could anyone do to stop it?

A railroad track ran behind our small church and each Sunday morning we could hear the whistle in the distance and then the wheels coming over the tracks. We became disturbed when we heard the cries coming from the train as it passed by. We realized that it was carrying Jews like cattle in the cars!

Week after week the whistle would blow. We dreaded to hear the sound of those wheels because we knew that we would hear the cries of the Jews en route to a death camp. Their screams tormented us.

We knew the time this train was coming and when we heard the whistle blow we began singing hymns. By the time the train came past our church we were singing at the top of our voices. If we heard the screams, we sang more loudly and soon we heard them no more.

Years have passed and no one talks about it anymore. But I still hear that train whistle in my sleep. God forgive me; forgive all of us who called ourselves Christians yet did nothing to intervene.[71]

It's sobering to think Christians would attempt to drown out desperate cries for help by amplifying the sound of their worship.

Read Amos 5:21-24. How did God feel about the people's worship? What did He say was missing from their worship?

The people were going through the act of worship but it wasn't sincere. What was missing was authenticity displayed through justice and righteousness.[72]

Before sharing the account of the German Christian, Erwin Lutzer asked his readers to consider this question as they continued reading: "What would I have done?"[73]

How many times have we watched news reports on television and switched channels—not because we didn't care but because we simply didn't know what to do? Maybe we felt hopeless and helpless or unsure how to reach out. Maybe we felt overwhelmed at the size of the problem because we didn't fully understand the magnitude of what we have to offer—the ability to bring a glimpse of heaven to earth.

> God wants us to turn down the music and listen for how we can make a difference. Look up Zechariah 7:9-10 and note how practical God is in directing us to administer His justice.

As with the Amos passage, God was not impressed with the people's religious activities. Their religiosity didn't match their character and behavior. So God told them what really mattered. In the NIV, verse 9 says to "administer true justice," and Zechariah explained what true justice is: showing compassion to one another; not oppressing people who are defenseless, weak, and in need of care; and not plotting evil against one another.

The purpose of having eternal spiritual lenses is to see people and then to do something—to help rescue them from spiritual darkness and alleviate their physical suffering. We are not to hide from the world but to go into all the world with the life-changing gospel. To make disciples. To express the love of Christ to the lost and lonely through our words and actions. We are to get equipped in the church so we can do the work of the ministry in the world—bringing glimpses of heaven to earth. Our time spent in Bible studies, worship, and fellowship needs to fuel us to go where we have been sent.

> Even if you know John 3:16 by heart, look it up and write verses 16-17 below.

God didn't send Jesus to destroy the world or humanity but to save it. To restore it. To transform it. When Jesus returns, there will be a new heaven and a new earth—all wrongs will be made right.

> The apostle John described the coming of the new heaven and the new earth. Look up Revelation 21:1 and write John's words.

John's words fulfill what Isaiah prophesied in Isaiah 65:17-18. Look up this passage and write it below.

From these verses, it's clear that this new heaven and earth will be our permanent and eternal home.

**ZOOM IN**
N.T. Wright, a leading New Testament scholar, wrote:

"What is promised after that interim period is a new bodily life within God's new world ('life after life after death'). I am constantly amazed that many contemporary Christians find this confusing. It was second nature to the early church and to many subsequent Christian generations.

It was what they believed and taught … God's plan is not to abandon this world, the world that he said was 'very good.' Rather, he intends to remake it. And when he does, he will raise all his people to new bodily life to live in it. That is the promise of the Christian gospel."[74]

God loves this world He created. And He loves His image-bearers who call it home. Read Genesis 1 and note every time you see the words "… and God saw that it was good."

How can God not love a world He created and called very good? And how can we not go into a world that He loves and is in need of His redemption and justice? Making an impact on a small percentage of the earth's population is better than not making an impact at all. As the parliamentarian Edmund Burke said, "The only thing necessary for the triumph of evil is for good men to do nothing."[75]

What is God calling you to do? Who is He calling you to reach? Is it local? Community-wide? Regional?

I understand we can't do everything, but I do believe we can all do something in our sphere of influence to bring a glimpse of heaven to earth.

# DAY 5

## *HERE AM I, LORD. SEND ME.*

"Why didn't you come sooner? If what you are telling me is true, if what you say about your God is true, then where were you?" Sonia demanded.

Her voice, rich with a beautiful Russian accent, was thick with emotion—almost taut from a simmering rage—and it pierced the depths of my heart.

I met Sonia more than ten years ago, right after we started A21. She challenged my good intentions. I was sitting in a circle of young women who had been rescued from sex trafficking, trying to encourage them and show them genuine love. But my words that seemed to penetrate their hearts only moments before were thrown right back at me with one explosive blow after another. Sonia was the bravest in the room because she dared to confront me, to voice what they were all thinking.

"Why didn't you come sooner?" She insisted. It was a raw and honest question that deserved a good answer.

Feeling the pressure of the moment, I searched for how to respond to her, to all of them. In the silence, no one moved. No one took their eyes off me. Sonia's heartbreaking cry for an answer reverberated like an echo in my head.

*Why didn't you come sooner?*

As I looked into her penetrating eyes, I could see the anguish they exposed, and my desperation to answer her softened into feelings of compassion I had never known. I shuddered at all she had shared. She was an eighteen-year-old who had been trapped in a room for one year, forced to service at least twenty-five men every day. Many of the women A21 helps are just like Sonia. All their stories of being poor, starving, and unable to feed or protect their families flooded my thoughts. They were easy prey for traffickers because they were so vulnerable.

Why hadn't I come sooner? How could I possibly help Sonia find forgiveness, healing, and restoration? *Jesus, help me. How should I answer her?*

Truthfully, I hadn't known of the horrific nightmare they were living. How could I intervene in something I didn't know even existed? I simply didn't know—until I did. And then I couldn't unknow it. That's when I responded. That's when Nick and I founded A21 in 2008. And God didn't just tell us to rescue victims of human trafficking; He gave us a vision for a complete work—from rescue to restoration. A21 gives victims healthcare, emotional support, housing, and education—and hope for a flourishing future.

But Sonia didn't care about any of that. Not that day. And I didn't offer any excuses. How could I? How dare I?

"I don't know," I stammered at last. "I don't know why I didn't come sooner." Such weak, small, light words for such a weighty question. "I am sorry. I am so sorry. Please forgive me."

The silence became even more pronounced. Time seemed to stop. And nothing else mattered to me at that moment but these girls and their despair—and the healing God could bring to them. Though the silence seemed to last for an eternity, I felt so clearly present, so tuned into the now.

"I want you to know that I have now heard your cries. I see you."

I turned to Maria. "I see you, Maria."

I turned to Sonia. "I see you, Sonia."

I looked intently at each girl seated at the table. "I see each of you. I hear you. I know you by name. I have come for each of you."

I wanted to see these girls as Jesus sees them—not as a sea of needs but as individuals He knows by name. They were girls made in the image of God, dearly loved by Him. These few represented thousands and thousands.

*Why didn't you come sooner?*

It's a question I have never forgotten, and one that has fueled my passion to reach the lost, the vulnerable, the poor, and the marginalized every day since.[76]

It's a question that has fueled my prayer since my early twenties when I began to understand what God had done in me and for me, and what He wanted to do for the broken and dying world around me. My prayer is founded in the words of Isaiah 6:8.

> Look up Isaiah 6:8. Write it below, then consider praying it with a heart of faith, passion, and commitment.

"Here am I, Lord. Send me," is a prayer I will never stop praying, because there is a world full of people crying out to be seen and to be found.

*Why didn't you come sooner?*

It was a painful question to answer, and one I believe God wants us to answer in our neighborhoods and communities.

> In light of all we've studied and discussed, what individuals or groups of people inside and outside your sphere of influence might be asking you this question in one way or another? As a way of acknowledging their value and God's desire to save them, write their names below.

> How do you, as the one God has sent to help them feel seen and loved, plan on answering them? Write all the ideas that come to mind.

As you put your thoughts on paper, commit them to the Lord. Ask for His wisdom and guidance on how you can help someone else experience the love, grace, and calling from God that you have. You've been seen, chosen, and sent, to help someone else be seen, chosen, and sent.

*Sent people don't stay; they go.*

Thank you for working through this study with me. I pray God has used it to do a work in you so He can do a work through you. I'm so proud of you, and I'm filled with hope and expectation for all God is going to do in the lives of the people you see every day, everywhere you go. You have new lenses now. You have 20/20 vision!

What a gift we can give. What a light we can be. Sent people don't stay; they go. So go!

Go, therefore, and make disciples of all nations, baptizing them in the name of the Father and of the Son and of the Holy Spirit, teaching them to observe everything I have commanded you. And remember, I am with you always, to the end of the age.
MATTHEW 28:19-20

## WEEK 7

# AS FAR AS THE
# EYE CAN SEE

# REFRAME YOUR VIEW

## WATCH
Watch Video Week 7, *The Exchange Zone*, and record your personal thoughts as you listen.

_____

_____

_____

_____

_____

_____

_____

_____

_____

_____

_____

_____

_____

_____

_____

_____

_____

## DISCUSS

I am so grateful you chose to come on this journey with me. I have loved running alongside you these past weeks, and now I am passing the baton to you. This is your time to run your race, in your lane, and go to the people in your world. Remember, we are part of a great cloud of witnesses (Heb. 12:1-2). We have a great heritage of faith. As you go, I know the Holy Spirit in you will be faithful to empower you to run with strength, courage, and endurance.

Pause for a moment. Take a look at your notes. What stood out to you from the video teaching?

"The future of the church ... hinges on how we pass the baton of faith from one generation to the next." Do you agree with this statement? Why or why not?

Do you feel the weight, the responsibility, of making sure to pass the baton of faith to the next generation? Explain.

What happens in our spiritual lives if we always seek the path of least resistance?

What's the biggest distraction that keeps you from running the race God has for you?

What are the most important lessons you learned or experienced through this study?

How has your perspective of others changed?

How has your perspective changed about how you can share Christ with others? What was it before journeying through this study? What is it now?

Do you feel more confident about meeting people outside your normal sphere of influence and befriending them? Is there someone you plan on inviting into your world who isn't a Christian? Explain.

Psalm 68:11 says, "The Lord gave the command; a great company of women brought the good news." The NIV translates the second part of the verse as "… and the women who proclaim it are a mighty throng." We are those women. We are part of a mighty throng. How exciting that we get to proclaim His good news everywhere we go.

## MOVE

It's time to make Jesus' last command our greatest priority. What does this mean to you? How are you committed to making this happen in your life?

## PRAY

Lord Jesus, help me to no longer be content to sit and soak in Your goodness while so many people around me are lost and broken. Thank You for seeing me, choosing me, and sending me into the world to share the good news of the gospel. May I go out with joy and be led forth in peace through the power of the Holy Spirit, knowing that You will do a great work in and through me. Here am I, Lord. Send me. In Jesus' name I pray. Amen.

# LEADER GUIDE

## A WORD TO THE LEADER

Thanks for taking on the responsibility of leading your group! I know you will be blessed and challenged. Below, find some tips to help you effectively lead the group study times:

## FORMAT

### GROUP SESSIONS

Each group session contains the following elements:

**GATHER:** This is a time to greet and welcome everyone, and then to get them talking. In the first session, you're provided with some icebreaker questions. In the subsequent sessions, you'll notice a list of questions to help participants review the previous week's personal study. Feel free to adapt, skip, or add questions according to the needs of your group.

**WATCH:** Each week you'll show a teaching video featuring Christine Caine. Encourage participants to take notes on the WATCH pages in their Bible study books.

**DISCUSS:** Each DISCUSS section begins and ends with a short paragraph. Feel free to use this content as you wish to summarize, encourage, or challenge. A list of questions is provided to help your group debrief what they heard on the video teaching. Again, feel free to adapt, skip, or

add questions as needed to foster discussion.

**MOVE:** This study is a call to action, so we've provided a section in the group time for participants to personally apply what they've heard and discussed. We suggest giving group members a few minutes of quiet to answer the challenges individually, followed by a time during which they partner up or gather in groups of three or four to share their commitments as a way to hold each other accountable.

**PRAY:** Close each session with prayer. But don't let this just be the rote bookend to the session. Be creative with how you lead this time and be sensitive to the Holy Spirit's direction. A written prayer that relates to the theme of the session is provided. You can use this however you wish to enhance or close the session.

## PERSONAL STUDY

Each session contains five days of personal study to help participants dig into God's Word for themselves. Encourage and challenge participants to complete each day of study, but give grace to those who may not be able to.

## PREPARE

**STUDY:** Make sure you've watched the teaching video and completed each week's personal study before the group session. Review the discussion questions and consider how best to lead your group through this time.

**PRAY:** Set aside time each week to pray for yourself and each member of your group.

**CONNECT:** Find ways to interact and stay engaged with each member of your group throughout the study. Make use of social media, email, and handwritten notes to encourage them. Continue these connections even after the study ends.

## SESSION 1

### GATHER

Welcome participants to the study and distribute Bible study books to each group member. Encourage discussion by asking the following questions:

- Why do you want to be a part of this study?

- What do you anticipate this study will be about?

- Share briefly how you first heard about Jesus and the gospel.

- Do you ever get the sense that God has called you to something greater—to do more for Him, make a bigger impact, be an agent of change? Explain.

- Leader: Call on someone to read Matthew 28:18-20.

- What thoughts and emotions stir in you when you hear those words from Jesus? Why?

- What do you hope this study will teach you?

### WATCH

Play the teaching video for Session 1. Encourage participants to take notes or jot down questions on the WATCH page (p. 8).

### DISCUSS

Use the information and questions found on page 9 to debrief the video teaching.

### MOVE

Briefly explain to your group members that this Bible study is not just for their personal spiritual growth but is a clear call to action. So, each group session will include a time for them to personally respond to specific challenges.

Invite group members to individually consider and answer the questions in the MOVE section. After a few moments, lead participants to partner up or get in groups of three or four to share how they responded to the MOVE questions as a way to hold each other accountable.

### PRAY

Close your session with a time of prayer.

## SESSION 2

### GATHER

Welcome participants back to the study. Use the following questions to review the previous week's personal study and prepare for the video teaching:

- What day of personal study had the most impact on you? Why?

- What are some things that keep you from really seeing the people in your line of sight?

- When you look at people, do you see them more through a lens of judgment or compassion? Explain.

- What does it mean to be compassionate? What was the latest opportunity you had to show compassion to someone? How did you respond?

- What does it mean to spiritually sleepwalk? Why do we so easily find ourselves in this condition? What are the consequences?

### WATCH

Play the teaching video for Session 2. Encourage participants to take notes or jot down questions on the WATCH page (p. 36).

### DISCUSS

Use the information and questions found on page 37 to debrief the video teaching.

### MOVE

Invite group members to individually consider and answer the questions in the MOVE section. After a few moments, lead participants to partner up or get in groups of three or four to share how they responded to the MOVE questions as a way to hold each other accountable.

### PRAY

Close your session with a time of prayer.

## SESSION 3

### GATHER

Welcome participants back to the study. Use the following questions to review the previous week's personal study and prepare for the video teaching:

- What day of personal study had the most impact on you? Why?

- We are chosen by God. What does that mean to you?

- Who were the people God used to reach you? How is God using you to reach others?

- How does God guide us to the lost? How have you seen God do that in your life?

- How are you currently being salt and light in your world?

- Are you currently participating in the harvest? If so, how are you seeing God work? If not, why not?

## WATCH

Play the teaching video for Session 3. Encourage participants to take notes or jot down questions on the WATCH page (p. 70).

## DISCUSS

Use the information and questions found on page 71 to debrief the video teaching.

## MOVE

Invite group members to individually consider and answer the questions in the MOVE section. After a few moments, lead participants to partner up or get in groups of three or four to share how they responded to the MOVE questions as a way to hold each other accountable.

## PRAY

Close your session with a time of prayer.

## SESSION 4

### GATHER

Welcome participants back to the study. Use the following questions to review the previous week's personal study and prepare for the video teaching:

- What day of personal study had the most impact on you? Why?

- Have you ever suffered from a spiritual blind spot? Explain.

- How does a broken heart or wounded soul affect your ability to serve and minister to others?

- Why is it such a struggle sometimes to keep your mind set on God and the things of God?

- For which neighbor in need is God calling you to cross the road? How do you need to reach out to this neighbor?

## WATCH

Play the teaching video for Session 4. Encourage participants to take notes or jot down questions on the WATCH page (p. 104).

## DISCUSS

Use the information and questions found on page 105 to debrief the video teaching.

## MOVE

Invite group members to individually consider and answer the questions in the MOVE section. After a few moments, lead participants to partner up or get in groups of three or four to share how they responded to the MOVE questions as a way to hold each other accountable.

## PRAY

Close your session with a time of prayer.

## SESSION 5

### GATHER

Welcome participants back to the study. Use the following questions to review the previous week's personal study and prepare for the video teaching:

- What day of personal study had the most impact on you? Why?

- What does it mean that we have an aroma? How do we smell to God? To others?

- Can people around you tell when you've been with Jesus? Explain.

- Why is it trouble if we get *doing* ahead of *being* in our spiritual lives?

- How does the Holy Spirit help us in our walk and ministry? Share a personal experience of how He has worked in you or through you.

- What's the key to producing spiritual fruit? Is this happening in your life? Explain.

### WATCH

Play the teaching video for Session 5. Encourage participants to take notes or jot down questions on the WATCH page (p. 136).

### DISCUSS

Use the information and questions found on page 137 to debrief the video teaching.

### MOVE

Invite group members to individually consider and answer the questions in the MOVE section. After a few moments, lead participants to partner up or get in groups of three or four to share how they responded to the MOVE questions as a way to hold each other accountable.

### PRAY

Close your session with a time of prayer.

## SESSION 6

### GATHER

Welcome participants back to the study. Use the following questions to review the previous week's personal study and prepare for the video teaching:

- What day of personal study had the most impact on you? Why?

- How do we see women play a prominent role in the New Testament?

- What women have influenced your spiritual life through the years? How?

- How have you seen words both build up and destroy? Why is the tone of our words so important?

- Why is your spiritual story a powerful way to share the gospel? When was the last time you shared it with someone?

## WATCH

Play the teaching video for Session 6. Encourage participants to take notes or jot down questions on the WATCH page (p. 166).

## DISCUSS

Use the information and questions found on page 167 to debrief the video teaching.

## MOVE

Invite group members to individually consider and answer the questions in the MOVE section. After a few moments, lead participants to partner up or get in groups of three or four to share how they responded to the MOVE questions as a way to hold each other accountable.

## PRAY

Close your session with a time of prayer.

## SESSION 7

### GATHER

Welcome participants back to the study. Use the following questions to review the previous week's personal study and prepare for the video teaching:

- What day of personal study had the most impact on you? Why?

- What is a spiritual bubble and why is it a hindrance to the work of Christ?

- How would you define "justice"? What does justice have to do with our carrying out the purpose of God?

- How would you explain the gospel to someone? Why is it important for you to know how to do that?

## WATCH

Play the teaching video for Session 7. Encourage participants to take notes or jot down questions on the WATCH page (p. 194).

## DISCUSS

Use the information and questions found on page 195 to debrief the video teaching.

## MOVE

Invite group members to individually consider and answer the questions in the MOVE section. After a few moments, lead participants to partner up or get in groups of three or four to share how they responded to the MOVE questions as a way to hold each other accountable.

Direct group members to look back over all the MOVE sections and note how they have followed through with their commitments and how they've seen God work. This could take place in the large group or the smaller accountability groups.

## PRAY

Close your session with a time of prayer.

# ACKNOWLEDGMENTS

It takes a tremendous team to get Bible studies like this into your hands. I will be forever grateful to all the people who helped make *20/20* an endearing work. I truly believe that teamwork makes the dream work.

To my husband, Nick, and to our girls, Catherine and Sophia: You make family life fun. Thank you for your endless love, sacrifice, patience, and support during the writing of this study. You are God's greatest gifts to me.

To our A21, Propel, Zoe Church, and Equip & Empower teams, volunteers, partners, and supporters: Changing the world with you one life at a time is the greatest privilege and honor of my life. You are the ones who make every endeavor possible.

To Elizabeth Prestwood: Your collaborative efforts helping me get my thoughts on paper are what turn ideas into reality and outlines into life-giving truths. Thank you for helping me unveil the vision in my heart. I could not do this without you. I thank God that He has graced me with such an amazing collaborative writer. You carried this project with me heart and soul.

To Rebekah Layton: You went above and beyond reading through every lesson and adding suggestions to help local church women be equipped and empowered. The contribution of your gift was invaluable. You are a gift.

To Beth Moore, Lisa Harper, and Priscilla Shirer, for coaching me as only veteran Bible study writers can. To Ann VosKamp, for being so willing to teach me about harvest time! Thank you all for your love and encouragement.

To the LifeWay Team: I am ever so grateful to have joined such a family of authors, editors, media, marketing, and publishing teams. To Faith Whatley, thank you for inviting me to the table and taking a risk. You are an outstanding leader full of wisdom and grace. To Michelle Hicks for your faith and vision. To Mike Wakefield and Elizabeth Hyndman, thank you for your years of combined wisdom and knowledge you put into the manuscript. To Sarah Doss and Emily Chadwell, thank you for your commitment to this project. To Heather Wetherington and Chelsea Waack, the cover and interior design said it all. To the LifeWay Video Team, you made filming this study a joy. Thank you.

To my Lord and Savior, Jesus Christ: He is everything.

# ENDNOTES

The bibliography for this study can be found at LifeWay.com/2020study.

1 "Divorce in the Old Testament." BibleStudyTools.com. https://www.bible-studytools.com/encyclopedias/isbe/divorce-in-the-old-testament.html (accessed March 21, 2019).

2 Bible Gateway. BibleGateway.com. https://www.biblegateway.com/resources/matthew-henry/Luke.7.36-Luke.7.49; (accessed March 21, 2019).

3 "Unseen," accessed April 30, 2019, https://en.oxforddictionaries.com/definition/unseen.

4 "Look," accessed March 21, 2019, https://en.oxforddictionaries.com/definition/look.

5 "See," accessed March 21, 2019, https://en.oxforddictionaries.com/definition/see.

6 Robert Stein, *The New American Commentary*, vol. 24, *Luke* (Nashville, TN: B&H Publishing Group, 2011).

7 Lisa Harper, *The Gospel of Mark* (Nashville, TN: LifeWay Press, 2016), 77.

8 James A. Brooks, *The New American Commentary*, vol. 23, *Mark* (Nashville, TN: Broadman Press, 1991).

9 "Blind," accessed March 21, 2019, https://en.oxforddictionaries.com/definition/blind.

10 "Compassion," *Bible Study Tools*, https://www.biblestudytools.com/lexicons/greek/nas/splagchnizomai.html

11 "Compassion Fatigue," accessed March 21, 2019, https://en.oxforddictionaries.com/definition/compassion_fatigue (accessed March 21, 2019).

12 To learn more about A21, visit their website: www.a21.org

13 Logan Block. "The Dangers of Sleepwalking." Sleepopolis.com. https://sleepopolis.com/education/the-dangers-of-sleepwalking (accessed March 21, 2019).

14 Adapted from a story first featured in Christine Caine's book, *Undaunted: Daring to do what God calls you to do* (Grand Rapids, MI: Zondervan, 2012, revised 2018).

15 "Chosen," accessed March 22, 2019, https://en.oxforddictionaries.com/definition/chosen.

16 Dr. James Strong, *"Eklektos,"* G1588, *The New Strong's Exhaustive Concordance of the Bible*. Available online at www.blueletterbible.org.

17 Rick Renner. "What God Thinks About You." Renner.org. https://renner.org/what-god-thinks-about-you/ (accessed March 25, 2019).

18 Richard L. Pratt, Jr, "1&2 Corinthians" in *Holman New Testament Commentary* (Nashville, TN: Broadman & Holman Publishers, 2000).

19 "Harvest," accessed March 25, 2019, https://en.oxforddictionaries.com/definition/harvest.

20 "Field of vision," accessed March 26, 2019, https://www.google.com/search?q=field+of+vision&oq=field+of+vision&aqs=chrome..69i57j0l5.1990j0j4&sourceid=chrome&ie=UTF-8.

21 "Worker," accessed March 26, 2019, https://en.oxforddictionaries.com/definition/worker.

22 Strong, *"Bethesda,"* G964.

23 Adapted from a story first featured in Christine Caine's book, *Unexpected: Leave Fear Behind, Move Forward in Faith, Embrace the Adventure* (Grand Rapids, MI: Zondervan, 2018).

24 "Blind spot," accessed March 26, 2019, https://en.oxforddictionaries.com/definition/blind_spot.

25 "How To Get Rid of Your Blind Spot." DefensiveDriving.com. https://www.defensivedriving.com/safe-driver-resources/how-to-get-rid-of-your-blind-spot/ (accessed March 26, 2019).

26 Max Knoblauch. "Here's United Airlines' adjusted 2017 pre-flight safety speech." Mashable.com. https://mashable.com/2017/04/10/united-airlines-pre-flight-safety-speech/#qsOqdN.eGmqT (accessed March 26, 2019).

27 This illustration was also used in Christine Caine's endorsement of the book, *Rethinking Human Trafficking* by Raleigh Sadler.

28 John MacArthur, "1-3 John" in *The MacArthur New Testament Commentary* (Chicago, IL: Moody Publishers, 2007).

29 Adapted from a story first featured in Christine Caine's book, *Unashamed: Drop the Baggage, Pick up Your Freedom, Fulfill Your Destiny* (Grand Rapids, MI: Zondervan, 2016).

30 John MacArthur, "Romans 9-16" in *The MacArthur New Testament Commentary* (Chicago, IL: Moody Publishers, 1994).

31 John MacArthur, "1 Corinthians" in *The MacArthur New Testament Commentary* (Chicago, IL: Moody Publishers, 1984).

32 Thomas R. Schreiner, *Tyndale New Testament Commentaries*, vol. 7, *1 Corinthians* (Downers Grove, IL: IVP Academic, 2007).

33 John Wilkinson. "The Way from Jerusalem to Jericho" in *The Biblical Archaeologist*, vol. 38, no. 1 (Alexandria, VA: ASOR, 1975). Available online at https://dokumen.tips/documents/the-way-from-jerusalem-to-jericho.html.

34 Adapted from a story first featured in Christine Caine's book, *Undaunted: Daring to do what God calls you to do* (Grand Rapids, MI: Zondervan, 2012, revised 2018).

35 Alexia Elejalde-Ruiz. "Scent branding catching on with retailers." ChicagoTribune.org. https://www.chicagotribune.com/business/ct-xpm-2014-04-20-ct-scent-brand-ing-0420-biz-20140420-story.html (accessed March 27, 2019).

36 "Pleasing Aroma," *Blue Letter Bible*, https://www.blueletterbible.org/search/search.cfm?Criteria=%22pleasing+aroma%22&t=CS-B#s=s_primary_0_1 (accessed 3/27/2019).

37 David Garland, *The New American Commentary*, vol. 29, *2 Corinthians* (Nashville, TN: Broadman & Holman Publishing Group, 1999).

38 Kenneth Schenck, *1 & 2 Corinthians: A Biblical Commentary in the Wesleyan Tradition* (Fishers, IN: Wesleyan Publishing House, 2006), 267.

39 Kathleen Lees. "Every Person has their Own Unique Scent." ScienceWorldReport.com. https://www.scienceworldreport.com/articles/11587/20131213/every-person-has-their-own-unique-scent.htm (accessed March 27, 2019).

40 "Witness," accessed March 27, 2019, https://en.oxforddictionaries.com/definition/witness.

41 Unites States Department of Justice. "Discovery." Justice.gov. https://www.justice.gov/usao/justice-101/discovery (accessed March 29, 2019).

42 Strong, *"Parakletos,"* G3875.

43 Beth Moore, *Living Beyond Yourself* (Nashville, TN: LifeWay Press, 1998).

44 "Love" in W.E. Vine's *Vine's Complete Expository Dictionary of Old and New Testament Words* (Nashville, TN: Thomas Nelson, 1996).

45 "Peace," Vine, *Vine's Complete Expository Dictionary of Old and New Testament Words*.

46 Strong, *"Makrothymia,"* G3115.

47 "Kindness," Vine, *Vine's Complete Expository Dictionary of Old and New Testament Words*.

48 "Goodness," Vine, *Vine's Complete Expository Dictionary of Old and New Testament Words*.

49 Strong, *"Pistis,"* G4102.

50 "Gentleness," Vine, *Vine's Complete Expository Dictionary of Old and New Testament Words*.

51 Strong, *"Egkrateia,"* G1466.

52 Adapted from a story first featured in Christine Caine's book, *Unexpected: Leave Fear Behind, Move Forward in Faith, Embrace*

*the Adventure* (Grand Rapids, MI: Zondervan, 2018).

53 Zhava Glaser. "Jesus and the Role of Women." JewsForJesus.org. https://jewsforjesus.org/publications/newsletter/newsletter-jun-1988/jesus-and-the-role-of-women/ (accessed March 29, 2019).

54 Claudia Hammond. "Prattle of the sexes: Do women talk more than men?" BBC.com. http://www.bbc.com/future/story/20131112-do-women-talk-more-than-men (accessed March 29, 2019).

55 The phrase "gossip the gospel" and its use throughout this week of study is inspired by Michael Green and his book, *Evangelism in the Early Church* (Grand Rapids, MI: Eerdmans, 1970), 173.

56 "Gossiping the Gospel." Faith-epc.org. http://faith-epc.org/wp-content/uploads/sermons/2015/06/4-Col-4-1-Pet-3-Gossiping-the-Gospel.pdf (accessed April 1, 2019).

57 "News," accessed April 1, 2019, https://en.oxforddictionaries.com/definition/news.

58 Strong, *"Zoe,"* G2222.

59 Strong, *"Shuwb,"* H7725.

60 "Restore," accessed April 1, 2019, in https://en.oxforddictionaries.com/definition/restore.

61 "Tone," accessed April 1, 2019, http://unabridged.merriam-webster.com/unabridged/tone?n=0&show=1&ref=unabridged&start=0&word=tone&expanded=no.

62 John Piper. "The Kingdom of God is Righteousness and Peace and Joy in the Holy Spirit." DesiringGod.org. https://www.desiringgod.org/messages/the-kingdom-of-god-is-righteousness-and-peace-and-joy-in-the-holy-spirit (accessed March 29, 2019).

63 "Kingdom," accessed April 2, 2019, https://www.merriam-webster.com/dictionary/kingdom.

64 Reggie McNeal, *Kingdom Come, Why We Must Give Up Our Obsession with Fixing the Church—and What We Must Do Instead* (Carol Stream, IL: Tyndale, 2015), 24-25.

65 "Justice," accessed April 2, 2019, https://www.dictionary.com/browse/justice.

66 David Griffin. "Justice and Righteousness." Ethos.org. http://www.ethos.org.au/online-resources/engage-mail/justice-and-righteousness (accessed April 2, 2019).

67 "Christians Have to Care About Injustice in the World." RelevantMagazine.com. ttps://relevantmagazine.com/current/nation/christians-have-care-about-injustice-world (accessed April 2, 2019).

68 "Roma (Gypsies) in Prewar Europe." Holocaust Encyclopedia. https://encyclopedia.ushmm.org/content/en/article/roma-gypsies-in-prewar-europe (accessed April 2, 2019).

69 David Dockery, ed., *Holman Concise Bible Commentary* (Nashville, TN: Holman Bible Publishers, 1998), 288.

70 Adapted from a story first featured in Christine Caine's book, *Undaunted: Daring to do what God calls you to do* (Grand Rapids, MI: Zondervan, 2012, revised 2018).

71 Erwin Lutzer, *When a Nation Forgets God: 7 Lessons We Must Learn from Nazi Germany* (Chicago, IL: Moody Publishers, 2009).

72 Billy K. Smith and Frank S. Page, *The New American Commentary*, vol. 19B, *Amos, Obadiah, Jonah* (Nashville, TN: Broadman & Holman Publishing Group, 1995).

73 *Ibid.*

74 N. T. Wright, *Simply Christian: Why Christianity Makes Sense* (San Francisco, CA: HarperOne, 2010), 218-219.

75 Edmund Burke. OpenCulture.com. http://www.openculture.com/2016/03/edmund-burkeon-in-action.html (accessed April 2, 2019).

76 Adapted from a story first featured in Christine Caine's book, *Undaunted: Daring to do what God calls you to do* (Grand Rapids, MI: Zondervan, 2012, revised 2018).